Richard

Happy 14th February 2006

with much love

the
BOOK of
aLCHEMY

FRANCIS MELVILLE

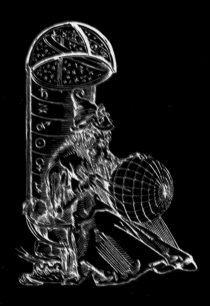

*That which is above is as that which
is below, and that which is below
is as that which is above.*

THE EMERALD TABLET

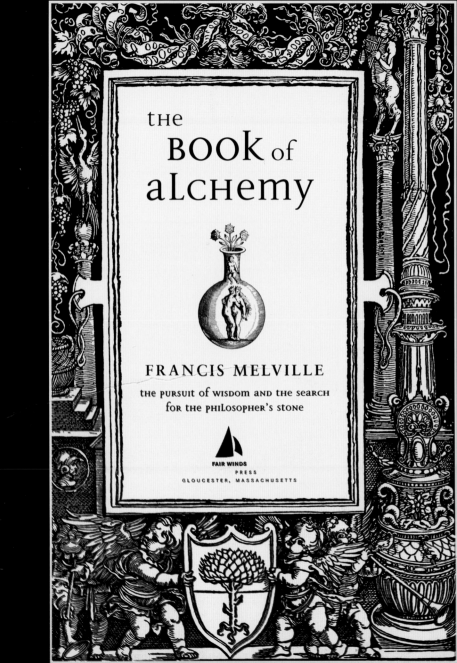

the
BOOK of
aLcHemy

FRANCIS MELVILLE

the pursuit of wisdom and the search
for the philosopher's stone

FAIR WINDS
PRESS
GLOUCESTER, MASSACHUSETTS

A QUARTO BOOK

10 9 8 7 6 5 4 3 2 1

ISBN 1-931412-27-8

Fair Winds Press
33 Commercial Street
Gloucester, MA 01930
USA

Sheridan House
112–116A Western Road
Hove
East Sussex BN3 1DD
England

Conceived, designed and produced by
Quarto Publishing plc
The Old Brewery
6 Blundell Street
London N7 9BH

QUAR.ALCH

Editor: Nadia Naqib
Art editor: Karla Jennings
Designer: Penny Dawes
Copy editor: Clare Haworth-Maden
Proofreader: Alice Tyler
Assistant art director: Penny Cobb
Photographer: Les Weis
Indexer: Dorothy Frame

Art director: Moira Clinch
Publisher: Piers Spence

Manufactured by
Universal Graphics Pte Ltd, Singapore
Printed by Midas Printing Ltd, China

NOTE

contents

INTRODUCTION

Alchemy has always been a mysterious, even obscure, art. Its origins are shrouded in mystery and steeped in myths and legends. Even the derivation of the word alchemy itself is uncertain. There are three main possibilities, each of which sheds light on the purpose and origins of alchemy. The first is from *Khem*, the native name of Egypt, with the Arabic prefix *al*. The second derives from the Greek word *chemeia*, meaning the art of casting metal, while the third is derived from *chumeia*, another Greek word, meaning the art of extracting juice or medicinal properties from plants. The first explanation has been the most widely held, but there is disagreement as to what Khem really means. It is usually thought to mean black, Egypt therefore being the Black Land, an allusion to the black alluvial silt that for millennia was borne down the Nile and annually flooded the flat lands of northern Egypt before the building of the Aswan Dam. Some scholars maintain that Khem is actually derived from a root meaning wise. Alchemy would therefore be the art from the Land of the Wise, or the wise art.

Whatever its origins, alchemy is a word that is familiar to most of us, and yet it remains one of the most mysterious of all the esoteric-wisdom traditions. Until recently, science historians have tended to consider alchemy as a forerunner of modern chemistry, and alchemists the deluded practitioners of an illusory pseudoscience, who nevertheless managed to establish some useful scientific facts in the course of their experiments. But what of all of the princes, saints, popes, and queens who have practiced this art? To say nothing of such eminent scientists as Isaac Newton, Robert Boyle, and Jan Van Helmont?

THE MACROCOSM AND THE MICROCOSM

*Via Dame Nature the Ape of Art receives the Invisible Fire
from the hand of God. Thus he has the tools with which
to ape nature and perform marvelous works.*

Goe forth little Booke in volume but small, Yet hast thou
in thee that is not in them All.
THE BREVIARY OF NATURALL PHILOSOPHY

MARIA THE JEWESS

The legendary alchemist Maria the Jewess, aka Maria
Prophetissa, indicates the mystical marriage of soul and
spirit, as symbolized by the commingling of the descending
water of heaven with the rising water of earth.

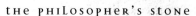

the philosopher's stone

The great bone of contention about the plausibility of alchemy is a mysterious substance called the *Philosopher's Stone*. Methods for confecting this "stone" provide the avowed basis of the great majority of alchemical texts. This "stone of the wise" is claimed to transmute base metal into the purest gold. Dream on, says the rational skeptic, and who can blame him or her? It is much easier to accept the idea that the true object of such a transmutation is the alchemist him- or herself, that the Philosopher's Stone actually represents perfect spiritual enlightenment. The attainment of enlightenment is equated with sainthood, the highest calling of all religions. Miracles appear to occur in the presence of saints. Could such miracles include transmutation?

What do alchemists themselves say about their art? The anonymous author of the influential *Sophic Hydrolith* ("Waterstone of the Wise," 1619) tells us that ". . . the practice of this Art enables us to understand, not merely the marvels of Nature, but the nature of God Himself. It shadows forth, in a wonderful manner . . . . all the articles of the Christian faith, and the reason why man must pass through much tribulation and anguish, and fall a prey to death, before he can rise again to a new life."

Alchemists recognize their art as a sacred science that unveils the secrets of nature, leading the sincere seeker to union with the divine. This union is achieved through preparing the Philosopher's Stone, which is said both to transmute base metals into gold and to be the Elixir of Immortality. A clue to the nature of the stone can be found in one of its alternative names— *Azoth*, from the (phonetic) Arabic *ez-zat*, meaning essence. Alchemists believe that there is an inner essence in humans that has been lost since the Fall, symbolized by the expulsion of Adam and Eve from the Garden of Eden. To rediscover this essence, free it from its bonds, and purify it is the Great Work of the alchemist.

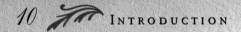
alchemy and mysticism

Many of the greatest alchemists teach us that in order to be worthy of finding the stone, the appropriate piety must be developed. As another adept, Basil Valentine, tells us,

"First, there should be the invocation of God, flowing from the depth of a pure and sincere heart, and a conscience which should be free from all ambition, hypocrisy, and vice, as also from all cognate faults, such as arrogance, boldness, pride, luxury, worldly vanity, oppression of the poor, and similar iniquities, which should all be rooted up out of the heart—that when a man appears before the Throne of Grace, to regain the health of his body, he may come with a conscience weeded of all tares, and be changed into a pure temple of God cleansed of all that defiles."

Such a call to sainthood, which is typical of alchemical literature, reveals that a certain mystical reverence is an essential part of an alchemist's makeup. Indeed, it could be said that laboratory alchemy represents the application of mystical religious principles to the physical plane to demonstrate that all is indeed one. The law of heaven is the law of nature. Chemistry appeared to take over from alchemy at a point when science was divorced from religion during the seventeenth century. Until that point they had been the same thing. For alchemists they still are.

exploring the mysteries of alchemy

We shall explore the religious and philosophical beliefs of alchemy in our attempt to understand it. We will look at some of its history, a few of its most significant personalities, and try to decipher the nature of the Great Work. As far as possible, we will allow the alchemists to speak for their art themselves. It should be pointed out that this will not be an exercise in cultural history. Classical alchemy is a living tradition practiced today by people on every continent. We do not have to set up a working laboratory in order to benefit from alchemy's astonishingly profound insights into the nature of reality and the nitty-gritties of the human soul. Many, possibly the majority, of genuine alchemists since the early seventeenth century have focused largely on the Inner Work of personal transformation. It is hoped that this book will serve as a sufficiently intriguing introduction to encourage some to explore deeper into the mysteries of alchemy.

LADY ALCHIMIA

*Lady Alchimia, Mistress of the Art, cradling the precious
quintessence, which has been separated from the earth
"gently and with great ingenuity"* (The Emerald Tablet).

SYMBOLISM IS AN INSPIRED FORM OF ARTISTIC IMPRESSION. IT IS THE CLOTHING
WHICH THE SPIRITUAL BORROWS FROM THE MATERIAL TO CONVEY MEANING

Alchemical Symbolism

The most immediately striking aspect of the great body of alchemical works is the extraordinary visual imagery with which many of them are illustrated. The examples chosen in this book give an impression of the powerful artistic expression used by alchemists to convey the secrets of their Art. Many are from the seventeenth century, when developments in printing allowed notable publishing houses to reproduce copperplate engravings with which to accompany alchemical texts. These illustrations often form the focal point of the work, even when the accompanying text seems at first glance to have little connection with them. Some important alchemical works, such as the *Mutus Liber* ("Mute Book"),1677, have no text at all, revealing their import only through pictures.

Alchemical imagery is extraordinarily rich. Apart from the Tarot, which is drawn from the same tradition, there is probably no other esoteric system with such a breadth of visual symbols. Symbolism is a form of inspired artistic impression. Symbols can activate responses that lie deep within us. In this sense they "work" whether we understand them intellectually or not. Engaging contemplatively with the symbolic pictures in this book can reveal more about the true nature of alchemy than reading works about it. The impact of an image may hit you in that thrilling way, both unnerving and inspiring, that shows you that you are known; that your story is intimately connected to the story; that the universe understands. This is alchemy.

You may find that what the alchemist is doing to the "base matter" is happening to you. Alchemical symbolism can produce subtle inner effects that bring about abrupt leaps of consciousness. It can awaken the dragons that guard the treasures of your soul. We must be careful not to antagonize them or they may tear us to pieces. You will notice that many of the symbolic themes involve the struggles of love and separation, death and resurrection. Alchemy shares these themes with Shamanism, Christianity, and the ancient mystery religions of the Mediterranean. The initiate is torn apart by conflicting forces, dying a symbolic, but psychologically very real, death, before being resurrected in a

state of grace. This brutal purification process is necessary to perfect the Stone, both chemically and spiritually.

Alchemical texts speak in symbolic riddles. In this book we will attempt to establish the principles on which they are based and divest some of alchemy's naked truths of its symbolic clothing. My interpretations are only to be thought of as suggestions. It is hoped that you will be armed with enough tools to find your own meaning.

KEY ALCHEMICAL THEMES

Emblems 1 and 2 (top left and right respectively) depict the four main stages of the Great Work. The snake in emblem 3 (bottom left) represents the unrefined three principles of sulfur, mercury, and salt, or salt, spirit, and body. The dragon in emblem 4 (bottom right) represents the dangerous volatile lower nature that the adept must transcend.

a BRIEF

HISTORY
OF THE ART

Western alchemy has a long and checkered history that stretches back into the mists of preantiquity. We will begin this historical section with a sketch of Hermes Trismegistus, the legendary founder of alchemy, and will follow the lines of transmission through the Islamic alchemists into medieval Europe and right up to the present day. We will plot the most important developments of the art during the course of the past two thousand years and will discover that alchemy is very much alive and kicking today, with modern alchemists rediscovering and successfully performing some of the most important and difficult works. Along the way, we will encounter some of the strangest, and most mysterious, episodes in the history of alchemy and will meet some of its most important practitioners.

SEEING THROUGH THE VEIL

The ecstatic pilgrim breaks through the veil of the material world, of which even the visible stars are a part, and perceives the glorious workings of the heavens.

"THRICE GREATEST" HERMES, OR HERMES TRISMEGISTUS IS TRADITIONALLY CONSIDERED TO HAVE BEEN A GREAT SAGE OF PREDELUVIAN EGYPT AND AN EARLY LINK IN THE CHAIN OF DIVINELY ILLUMINATED ADEPTS THAT INCLUDES ZOROASTER, ENOCH, MOSES, PYTHAGORAS, AND PLATO

HERMES TRISMEGISTUS

"Thrice Greatest" Hermes, or Hermes Trismegistus, is the legendary genius of alchemy, which is why alchemists often refer to themselves as sons of Hermes and there are enough legends surrounding his identity to fill a whole book. We shall consider two of his most significant aspects.

THOTH

The Ancient Egyptians knew Hermes Trismegistus as Thoth, the divine personification of wisdom, whom they portrayed as the ibis-headed scribe of the gods; the inventor of hieroglyphics; patron of the sacred sciences of geometry, mathematics, astronomy, and medicine, but, above all, alchemy. Thoth exists at every level of being. He serves the gods, but also preceded them. Indeed, he brought them into being. He is the self-creating arch-magician, the word of God in action. He has but to name a thing and it springs into life, "clothed with being."

THE EGYPTIAN HERMES

The Greeks identified their god Hermes as being an aspect of Thoth, which is why they named him Hermes Trismegistus ("Thrice Greatest") in recognition of his status, although legend also has it that there were three separate historical Hermes. The Greek Hermes is the messenger of the gods, who mediates between heaven, above, and earth, below. He is the ambivalent god of the crossroads, being both guide and trickster and patron of both merchants and thieves. The Roman equivalent of Hermes is Mercury, and alchemists often refer to Hermes Trismegistus as Mercury or Mercurius. As we shall see, the alchemists apply the word mercury to so many different things that it exemplifies the great riddle of life.

THE HERMETICA

Hermes Trismegistus is accredited with a body of writing known as the *Hermetica*, or *Corpus Hermeticum*. These texts were generally believed to be very ancient indeed. It was not until the seventeenth century that it was established that the texts, as they have come down to us, were written down in Alexandria during the first three centuries of the Christian era, although they may have been elaborations upon earlier manuscripts. Some of these writings were translated by Arab scholars from Greek and Coptic manuscripts and were introduced into Europe via the Moors of Spain during the twelfth century. The main body, however, was not translated until 1471, when Cosimo de Medici, the great patron of the Florentine Renaissance, instructed Marsilio Ficino to interrupt his translations of Plato to translate into Latin a Greek set of the *Hermetica* that Cosimo had obtained from Byzantium.

MARRIAGE OF SOL AND LUNA

Hermes indicates the marriage of Sol and Luna. The creative fire that forges the union of the two polarities gives rise to the manifest universe.

The recent development of printing allowed for the *Hermetica's* swift dispensation throughout Europe. The impact of the *Hermetica* on Renaissance philosophy was enormous. Here was an ancient body of theological, philosophical, scientific, and medical writings of extraordinary beauty, intellectual power, and spiritual authority, in which Jews, Christians, and Muslims could find confirmations, amplifications, and refinements of their own sacred teachings. The creation myth becomes a much richer, more detailed, and expressive allegory, an awesome alchemical process. Hermes describes humans as the "great miracle," capable of achieving godhood as individuals by transcending the states of being that separate them from the divine. Humans are dignified as being truly made in the image of God, being the microcosms that

THE EMERALD TABLET

The Alchemical Mountain contains the secrets of the Emerald Tablet. From the mountain pour forth the primary elements of fire and water. The rural setting dotted with churches and other signs of human life is typical of 17th-century alchemical emblems.

reflect the macrocosm. Everything in creation finds its reflection in humans, who therefore have at their disposal all the tools that they need to achieve their divine destiny, should they choose to accept it.

the emerald tablet

The most famous text attributed to Hermes Trismegistus is *The Emerald Tablet*, or *Tabula Smaragdina*. There are as many legends surrounding it as there are of Hermes himself. Inscribed on green stone, it is variously said to have been discovered by Sara, the wife of Abraham, Alexander the Great, or the first-century sage, Apollonius of Tyana. The earliest-known version of it is to be found in a text by the

eighth-century Islamic alchemist Jabir ibn
Hayyan ("Second Book of the Elements of
Foundation," Holmyard), who credits
Apollonius as his source. Medieval Latin
versions of *The Emerald Tablet* can be
traced to twelfth-century Moorish Spain,
making it the first Hermetic text to reach the
West. To the uninitiated, *The Emerald Tablet*
appears to be a confusingly cryptic riddle, but it
has always been held in the highest regard by true
alchemists as the most perfect précis of the creative
principles of the universe. The following version is based
on various Latin and English translations.

> *This is the truth, the whole and certain truth,*
> *without a word of a lie.*
>
> *That which is above is as that which is below,*
> *And that which is below is as that which is above.*
> *Thus are accomplished the miracles of the One.*
>
> *And as all things come from the One, through the mediation of the*
> *One, So all things are created by this One Thing through adaptation.*
>
> *Its father is the Sun; its mother the Moon.*
> *The Wind bears it in its belly; the Earth nurtures it.*
>
> *It engenders all the wonders of the Universe.*
>
> *Its power is complete when it is turned to Earth.*
>
> *Separate the Earth from Fire, the subtle from the gross,*
> *Gently and with great ingenuity.*
>
> *It ascends from Earth to Heaven and descends again to Earth,*
> *Combining the power of above and below.*
>
> *Thus you will achieve the glory of the Universe*
> *And all obscurity will flee from you.*
>
> *This is the power of all powers,*

For it overcomes every subtle thing
And penetrates every solid thing.

Thus was all the world created.

And thus are marvelous works to come,
For this is the process.

Therefore am I called Thrice-greatest Hermes,
For I am master of the three principles of
universal wisdom.

This concludes what I have to say
about the work of the Sun.

THE CADUCEUS

The Wand of Hermes, also known as the *caduceus*, consists
of two serpents entwined around a central pillar or wand.
The wand is often surmounted by wings, a crown, or a
fleur-de-lis.

Derived from a word meaning "herald," and borne by Hermes in his
role as celestial herald, the caduceus is itself an important message for

humanity. The coupling snakes represent all of
the opposing principles at play in the manifest
universe: male/female, Sun/Moon, soul/spirit,
or, in alchemical terminology, *Sol/Luna* and
sulfur/mercury. The central pillar represents
the axis between heaven and earth, the
above and the below. The wings represent
transcendence, the crown, divine authority,
while the fleur-de-lis is the Trinity.

The caduceus is an ancient symbol. The
earliest known version is about five thousand
years old. It is a symbol of peace, protection,
and healing, and is used to this day as a
medical symbol. Above all, it is a symbol of

unity achieved through the reconciliation of
opposites. It appears in many traditions and
finds one of its most significant expressions in
Indian yoga.

aLcHeMy aND yoĢa

Yoga is a Hindu system of philosophy devoted to
the mystical union of the self with the supreme
being. Because the aims of alchemy and yoga are
the same, alchemy is often described as "Western
yoga." Yoga employs physical and mental
exercises with which to achieve a state of
complete awareness and tranquillity. It identifies
subtle energy channels, known as *nadis*, within
the body. Two of these nadis spiral around a central
channel that runs within the spinal cord. The red
nadi, called *pingala*, is masculine, solar, and
warming by nature and its course runs from the left
testicle (or the left side of the vulva in women) to the
right nostril. The nature of the light-blue nadi, called

THE CHAKRAS

The two nadis, *the* pingala *and the* ida
wind around the central axis within the
subtle body. The chakras represent the
points at which the nadis cross.

ida, is opposite to that of pingala: it is feminine, lunar, and cooling and its course runs from the
right testicle (or the right side of the vulva) to the left nostril. The central column, called
susumna, contains within itself the equivalents of both pingala and ida. At its core is the
Brahma-nadi, the channel for supreme consciousness within the individual.

The parallels between the nadis and the caduceus are immediately apparent. Pingala and
ida correspond to sulfur and mercury, the masculine and feminine principles within all of us,
regardless of our gender. The Brahma-nadi equates to the secret fire in alchemy, which
alchemists seek to locate both within themselves and within the substances that they work with.
The points at which the nadis cross are energy centers within the body known as *chakras*. By
bringing pingala and ida into conscious balance, the yogin seeks to awaken the serpent power
(*Kundalini*), the coiled energy that "sleeps" at the base of the spine. When awakened, this energy
rises up the susumna nadi and opens the chakras. When the serpent power reaches the highest
chakra, the yogin experiences the bliss of the supreme consciousness of Brahman, the
indestructible, absolute consciousness of the universe.

This is one of the great open secrets of alchemy: the wand that Hermes holds in his hands is the means of attaining union with the absolute. Nevertheless, this is not easily accomplished and takes sustained attention, practice, commitment, and faith. The way to begin is consciously to connect with the sulfur–mercury/pingala–ida channels within yourself. You can do this using a combination of breathing exercises and visualization.

the wind carries it in its belly

To begin, sit comfortably, hold your back straight, relax, and breathe regularly. Now start to focus on the chakras by breathing into the areas of the body that are marked on the chart, starting with the lowest chakra for a few breaths and then gradually moving up your spine. You may not directly sense these zones within your body at first, but after a few days the exercise will become familiar, the chakras will start to respond, and you will be able to feel them.

After breathing into the chakras, focus your attention on inhaling through your right nostril, if you are a man, or left nostril, if you are a woman, closing the other nostril with a finger if this helps. Inhale from the bottom of your lungs and imagine that your breath is following the course of the pingala or sulfur channel, if you are a man, or the ida or mercury channel, if you are a woman. Then switch your attention to your other nostril and allow your breath to follow the course of the opposite channel. Practice doing this for a few minutes twice a day. You will soon be able to breathe from the bottom of the channels and will feel the energy following your breath and weaving through the chakras.

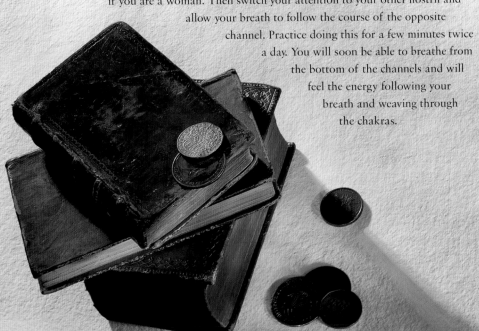

Next, try focusing on both of the snake-power channels at the same time. When you can imagine the two channels of energy rising simultaneously, and can feel them flowing through your energized chakras, you will be well on the way to achieving inner balance. You should bear in mind, however, that this is a powerful exercise that is likely to release blocked energy, in the form of emotions and tensions, within the body. Because this release can be quite upsetting, be gentle with yourself and do not force things. Never attempt these exercises while under the influence of psychoactive drugs or else you will risk suffering potentially severe setbacks. Have faith. Each breath that you take in is an inspiration, full of divine energy. Each breath that you release is an expiration, a death, a surrendering of used energy.

THE HERMETIC ART ENTERED EASILY INTO THE SPIRITUAL WORLD OF ISLAM. THE LATTER WAS ALWAYS READY IN PRINCIPLE TO LEARN FROM ANY PRE-ISLAMIC ART THAT FELL WITHIN THE RUBRIC OF *HIKMAH* ("WISDOM"), AS THE BEQUEST OF EARLIER PROPHETS

ISLAMIC ALCHEMY

Islam inherited the geographical empire carved out centuries earlier by Alexander the Great, but this empire's greatest treasure, the great library of Alexandria had long since perished. Despite this earlier loss, the phoenix of Hermetic wisdom was to rise again unexpectedly from the fertile soil of Islam. Within decades of the Prophet's death the most important works on philosophy, mathematics, medicine, astronomy, indeed all areas of learning, were being translated, primarily from Greek, into Arabic. Islam soon showed itself to be devoted to culture and learning, with enlightened rulers such as the Caliph of Baghdad Harun al-Rashid (764–809) patronizing scholars and establishing academies all over what had become a great empire stretching from the Pyrenees to the Indus.

AVICENNA, "PRINCE OF PHYSICIANS"

The Persian alchemist Avicenna indicates how the volatile can be fixed and the fixed made volatile. The book under his arm is probably the Book of Remedy, *his greatest alchemical work.*

khalid ibn yazid

Interest in alchemy was right at the forefront of Islam's cultural revolution. Indeed the very first books to be translated into Arabic were Greek and Coptic works on alchemy. These were translated by Greek scholars in Damascus for Prince Khalid ibn Yazid around 690 A.D. Khalid was in line to become Caliph, the most powerful man in Islam, but he chose instead to devote his life to learning. He went on to study the Art under a Christian alchemist called Morienus of Alexandria, who is said to have performed a successful transmutation for him. Several alchemical texts attributed to Khalid have survived, including *The Paradise of Wisdom*.

jabir ibn hayyan

Islam's greatest alchemist was Jabir ibn Hayyan (c.721–815), a disciple of the Imam Ja'far As-Sadiq, a direct descendant of the Prophet himself. Jabir was famed for his medicinal elixirs, produced as court alchemist to Harun al-Rashid. The famous caliph's court in Baghdad represented the epitome of Arabian culture and romance. This is the Baghdad of the Arabian Nights—Aladdin, genies, magic, mystery, and intrigue. Ancient folklore and old magic combined with Hermetism and Islamic mysticism to produce a potent new alchemy. Jabir derived further inspiration from China. Among the precious goods carried along the Silk Route were some of the treasures of Chinese alchemy, including the magic square of the Ming Tang, the Temple of Light.

the magic square

The magic square consisted of nine numbers, with the number five in the center. Jabir derived the numbers one, three, five, eight, seventeen, and twenty-eight from the square and applied these numbers to his understanding of the alchemical elements and their successful manipulation. His mystical interpretation of this magic square provided the basis of his Theory of Balance, which is considered one of Jabir's most important contributions to the Art. Jabir also adopted the Chinese concept of mercury being the soul of metals and introduced the sulfur–mercury theory which we will explore later.

AVICENNA

This seal, one of 160 emblems of celebrated Hermetic figures in the Basilica philosophica of J. D. Mylius, commemorates the Persian alchemist Avicenna. The inscription reads "The eagle flying through the air and the toad walking on the ground is the Magistery."

Jabir's work became the foundation stone for Western alchemy some four centuries later. Known in the West as Geber, Jabir wrote many works on alchemy, although most of those attributed to him were written by disciples as much as seven hundred years after his death. It is in one of Jabir's own works that we find the first reference to the Emerald Tablet. His name entered the vernacular in the form of "gibberish"—an indication of just how complex and riddling his writing can appear. After his death his laboratory was found to contain a solid gold mortar weighing two pounds.

RHAZES AND AVICENNA

Other Muslim alchemists whose work was of enduring influence include al-Razi and Ibn Sina, known in the West as Rhazes and Avicenna respectively. Rhazes (c.860–925) was a merchant's son from Ray in Persia, who gave up a life as a musician to devote himself to philosophy and medicine. He studied in Baghdad and returned a man of science, critical of both fanaticism and mysticism, showing perhaps a little too much of the modern world's failure to distinguish superstition from spirituality. He added salt as a third principle to Jabir's mercury-sulfur theory. Rhazes remained an authority at European universities into the seventeenth century. He wrote some twenty books on alchemy and classified a great number of substances, medicines, apparatus, and processes. He famously declared "Who knows not chemistry does not deserve the name of philosopher."

4	9	2
3	5	7
8	1	6

THE MAGIC SQUARE OF JABIR

This is known as a square of order three, ascribed in Hermetic magic to Saturn. Each line adds up to 15 and the sum of all the numbers is 45. Jabir derived the numbers one, three, five, eight, seventeen, and twenty-eight from the square after separating the gnomon (the remainder of a square after the removal of a similar square containing one of its corners).

Avicenna (980–1037), another Persian, was born in the old Silk Route city of Bokhara. He was a prodigious intellect and, having out learned his tutors at an early age, he devoted himself to the private study of medicine. By the age of seventeen he was physician to a prince and went on to lead an enormously colorful and productive life. His massive *Canon of Medicine* earned him the title "Prince of Physicians" and made him an oracular authority until deep into the Renaissance. His greatest alchemical work is the *Book of the Remedy*, in which he concurs with Jabir and Rhazes on the generation of metals, but expresses skepticism about transmutation.

For all his brilliance, Avicenna lacked a certain magical understanding. Like Rhazes he was more a scholar than a seer.

With the benefit of hindsight it seems more appropriate to consider both Rhazes and Avicenna as proto-chemists, their concern was with the chemical science of their day rather than with the spiritual art of transmutation. Perhaps a better, though less well known, example of an Islamic alchemist is the thirteenth-century Abu'l Qasim al-Iraqi. His *Book of Knowledge Acquired Concerning the Cultivation of Gold* is a masterly summary of Islamic alchemy in the tradition of Jabir ibn Hayyan. What Islamic alchemists such as Jabir and Abu'l Qasim had in common was an affinity with the Hermetic and Platonic mysticism of the Greeks, with whom they shared a gnostic vision of Unity that called them to seek perfection through purification and knowledge of the Divine.

MORIENUS

Morienus, the teacher of Prince Khalid, admonishes a man stuck in the dungheap of ignorance. The Prime Matter must be liberated from such dross. The falling man in the background shows that the Tower of Alchemy cannot be ascended without the Ladder of the Wise.

THE INTRODUCTION OF CLASSICAL GREEK PHILOSOPHY INTO MEDIEVAL EUROPE BY
THE MOORS LED TO THE RENAISSANCE. ALCHEMICAL TEXTS ENTERED BY THE SAME
ROUTE, INITIATING A GOLDRUSH THAT CONTINUED INTO THE SEVENTEENTH CENTURY

IN PURSUIT
OF GOLD

Arab culture and knowledge began to be transmitted to
Europe after the Islamic Moors under Tarik ibn Zayid
invaded Spain in A.D 711 and built three great
universities at Toledo, Cordoba, and Seville.

Gnostic and Neo-Platonic works were brought to
France during the ninth century, where they were
translated by Johannes Scotus Erigena, a Scottish mystic
from Ireland. Christian mysticism subsequently re-emerged as the
mystery of the Holy Grail. However, despite its practice among the
Ancient Greeks, alchemy was generally unknown in Europe prior to the Moorish invasions.
After Toledo was retaken from the Moors in 1105, Archbishop Raymond founded the College of
Translators there for the purpose of translating Arabic works for Europeans. The earliest-known
translation of Arabian alchemy into Latin was Englishman Robert of Chester's translation of
The Book of the Composition of Alchemy, by Morienus, in 1144. Robert was also the first to
translate the Koran and the Arabian form of mathematics known as algebra. His most
influential work was the translation of *The Emerald Tablet* from Jabir's writing. Such scholars as
Gerard of Cremona, in Lombardy, Adelard of Bath, Roger of Hereford, and Maimonides the
Jew increasingly revealed the vastness of Arabic knowledge to Europeans. As a result, a wave of
alchemical studies was ignited throughout Europe.

Some of the greatest minds of the time took up alchemy. These included the German bishop
Albertus Magnus, who was born in Swabia in 1193, and his famous student, Saint Thomas
Aquinas; the Franciscan friar Roger Bacon, who was born in Somerset, England, in 1214; and
Arnold of Villanova, physician to kings and popes, who was born in Valencia, Spain, in 1235.

ATHANOR

An alchemist and his
assistant at work in
the laboratory. In the
middle ground is the
athanor, the alchemical
furnace. Many alchemists
were blacksmiths, as the
forge and anvil in this
emblem suggest.

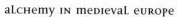

aLcHeMY IN MeDIeVaL euRope

The idea of the Philosopher's Stone also exerted
a powerful hold on the less lofty aspects of the
medieval mind, attracting the greedy, gullible, and
dishonest, who were only interested in material
gold. Such "puffers" (being either fire-blowers or
puffed up with conceit) led the art into disrepute,
but their materialist emphasis served to protect
alchemy from being branded heretical by the
Roman Catholic Church. Even so, the production
of alchemical gold from powder that had fallen
into unworthy hands or, more commonly, cleverly
faked gold, reached such levels that in 1317 Pope
John XXII issued a decree prohibiting the practice of
alchemy. In spite of royal and papal bans and the fraud
and failures associated with gold-making, alchemists
continued to study and publish throughout Europe. A
significant number of alchemists were members of the clergy,
including abbots, bishops, and cardinals. Many kings and princes were also
alchemists, who either had their own alchemical laboratories or paid for those of the many
alchemists whom they hired. It was not uncommon for alchemists to be extremely learned
men, many of them physicians, who traveled widely in search of alchemical knowledge at a
time when such travel was dangerous. What drove these people was a belief in the sacred,
transformative value of the art and also the tantalizing rumors of genuine transmutations.

THe TRansMuTaTion of van HeLMonT

The case of Van Helmont is worth relating here because it is a typical example that
even hardened skeptics often find hard to dismiss out of hand. Jan Baptista Van Helmont
(1577–1644) was a pioneering chemist and physician. He was a follower of Paracelsus (see
pages 34 to 37) and shared his mystical view of nature. He was sympathetic to alchemical
ideas, but had expressed himself skeptical of transmutation. One day he was visited by a
stranger who engaged him in a conversation about the Philosopher's Stone. Van Helmont
challenged his assumptions, whereupon the stranger produced a container full of a powder,
of which he gave Van Helmont a tiny amount. The stranger told him how to use the powder
and then made ready to leave. When Van Helmont expressed surprise that he did not wish to
observe the outcome of the operation, the stranger replied that the outcome was assured. Van

Helmont asked him why he had sought him out in this way. "To convince an illustrious scientist whose work does honor to his country," replied the stranger, and left. Van Helmont followed the stranger's instructions to the letter and successfully performed a transmutation.

Such accounts of strangers performing transmutations in front of reliable witnesses, or providing specimens of "projecting powder" to be proven in their absence, persisted throughout the seventeenth and eighteenth centuries. Several coins and medals made from alchemical gold are preserved in museums and private collections in Europe. Who the true adepts were, and how they achieved the Philosopher's Stone, remains a mystery to all but perhaps a very few.

IN PURSUIT OF THE STONE

A medieval puffer and his confused assistant engaged in pursuit of the Philosopher's Stone. Countless honest, if deluded, practitioners ruined themselves in their hopeful quest. Many must have fallen victim to the poisonous fumes of mercury.

THE SERPENT OR DRAGON FORMING A CIRCLE WITH ITS TAIL IN ITS
MOUTH IS AN ANCIENT REPRESENTATION OF THE SELF-SUSTAINING
NATURE OF LIFE. IT FEEDS OFF ITSELF, DESTROYING, FERTILIZING,
AND CREATING IN AN ETERNAL CYCLE

THE OUROBOROS

The Greek sage Epicurus wrote "The All was from the beginning like an egg, with the serpent as the tight band or circle round it." The ouroboros is both serpent and egg. It is spirit waiting to be ensouled; God the Mother ready to receive the inseminating light of God the Father; the potential of Creation prior to realization. This aspect of the ouroboros is described in the Tao te Ching.

The ouroboros is *prima materia*, the "first matter" from which all things are born. This is the essential material that the alchemist must work with to create the Philosopher's Stone. The circle represents the movement of Divine Energy away from and back toward itself— "My end is my beginning."

The double ouroboros combines two serpents, one winged. Each bites the tail of the other to form a circle. This symbol represents the great alchemical dictum *Solve et Coagula*, meaning "dissolve the body and coagulate the spirit." The lower, wingless serpent is the body, the gross matter or unenlightened individual that must be dissolved. The three horns on its head represent the three inherent philosophical principles— soul, spirit, and body—that must be purified. The upper serpent is the spirit. Its wings denote its elusive, volatile quality, which must be coagulated—fixed—in order to be embodied. The crown on its head

There is a mysterious thing
That existed before Heaven and Earth.
Silent and empty,
Alone and unchanging,
Ceaselessly turning,
It is the Mother of All Things.

If I must, I'll call it "Great."
Greatness entails transcendence.
Transcendence entails going beyond.
Going beyond entails return to the
beginning.

TAO TE CHING XXV,
AUTHOR'S INTERPOLATION

reveals its divine nature. This symbol represents the union of opposites, an alchemical yin-yang. It is the *circulatio*, or circulation, in which the dissolved matter continually evaporates and recondenses, freeing and reintegrating the spirit, which in turn exalts the matter or body. The work is completed when "That which is above is as that which is below," namely when the two serpents are fully integrated as One Thing. The perfected serpent represents the Philosopher's Stone. It retains the crown of divinity and is wingless, fixed, and unchanging in its perfection.

CIRCLE OF LIFE

The ouroboros symbolizes life on every level—the macrocosm and the microcosm, the universal and the individual.

In comparison to Dame Nature the alchemist is a blind, benighted old man. Her footprints are clear enough, but he needs a lamp, stick, and spectacles to follow them. The imitation of Nature, perceived as a conscious, living force, is a recurrent theme in alchemy.

PARACELSUS THE GREAT

ONE OF THE MOST REMARKABLE MEN
OF HIS AGE, THE ENIGMATIC AND
CONTRADICTORY THEOPHRASTUS
BOMBASTUS VON HOHENHEIM,
KNOWN AS PARACELSUS, REVOLUTIONIZED
BOTH MEDICINE AND ALCHEMY AND
SOWED THE SEEDS OF HOMEOPATHY.

Born in Switzerland in 1493,
Paracelsus received his early
education from his physician father.
His mother died when he was young,
and he moved with his father to a
mining district in Carinthia, in Austria,
where he attended the local school and
shared his father's interest in alchemy. At
the age of sixteen he attended university
before spending some time with Johannes
Trithemius, Abbot of Sponheim, one of
the greatest mages of the sixteenth century.
What he learned from Trithemius would help

to forge an undying faith in alchemy and the conscious forces of nature. Paracelsus then worked at the mines of a wealthy alchemist in the Tyrol. There he learned the physical properties of ores and metals, studied extraction and purification, and noted the curative effects of mineral waters. He observed the accidents and diseases that befell the miners and decided to become a physician.

Sixteenth-century physicians tended to live in ivory towers of scholasticism, studying the texts of ancient authorities and concerning themselves entirely with theory. They seldom dealt with patients, and had little or no practical experience. This may have suited the physician, but seldom the patient. It was not the kind of physician that Paracelsus wished to become.

Upon receiving his doctorate from the University of Ferrara, in Italy, Paracelsus traveled all over Europe and beyond for seven years, often by foot. Rejecting university libraries, he chose instead to "read in Nature's book." He learned all that he could of medical folklore and plant-cunning from Gypsies and midwives, and much else besides from all the people with whom he engaged in countries as diverse as England, Spain, Italy, Scandinavia, Portugal, Turkey, and Russia.

trials and tribulations

Paracelsus eventually returned to Switzerland, where he was received with great honor, being made a town physician in 1527. His legendary cures established his reputation, but he soon outraged his peers by mocking and insulting them and lecturing in German rather than the time-honored Latin. When he went as far as burning books in public, the faculty at the University of Basle tried, unsuccessfully, to stop him from lecturing. He made further enemies among the apothecaries, whom he accused of exploiting the sick. The situation reached a critical point when a rich prelate refused to pay Paracelsus the huge sum that he had promised him for a cure. Paracelsus sued him. When the court awarded him just a fraction of his fee, he published a scathing attack on its integrity, a punishable offence. In peril of imprisonment, Paracelsus slipped out of the city of Basle, never to return.

Paracelsus never achieved such a prominent position again and returned to a life of wandering. During his remaining years, he wrote, or dictated, a great body of work. Only his two books on surgery were published during his lifetime (in 1536), but they were widely acclaimed and remained authorities for many years. By this time Paracelsus had re-established his reputation and was invited in 1540 to settle in Salzburg, Austria. But just when it seemed that he might find some rest he died, probably murdered by his enemies.

IDEAS, BELIEFS, AND DOCTRINES

Paracelsus understood that just as animals instinctively recognize the virtues of plants, so humans can re-develop an instinctive rapport with nature, which can then transmit its secrets to them. Humans can come to know the true nature of things not by reading about them, or even thinking about them, but by *being with* them. Paracelsus perceived nature as a conscious, mystical, living force that is able to engage directly with people whose hearts and souls are open. This appreciation is true alchemy: the ability to identify with something on the most intimate level, allowing both to be all that they can be.

Paracelsus developed the doctrine of signatures, which describes how nature reveals itself through its signs. The shape or color of a plant, for example, can indicate its medicinal use. For those able to read it, nature is an open book, and Paracelsus tells us how: "through prayer, faith, and imagination. Prayer, according to Paracelsus, is a strong desire and aspiration for that which is good. We must seek and knock and thereby ask the Omnipotent Power within ourselves, and remind it of its promises and keep it awake, and if we do this in the proper form and with a pure and sincere heart, we shall receive that for which we ask, and find that which we seek, and the doors of the Eternal that have been closed before us will be opened." Faith, Paracelsus tells us, is not mere belief, but an "unwavering confidence" based upon *knowing*, "a faith that may move mountains and throw them into the ocean, and to which everything is possible. Faith is a luminous star that leads the honest seeker into the mysteries of Nature. You must seek your point of gravity in God, and put your trust in an honest, divine, sincere, and strong faith and cling to it with your whole heart, soul, sense, and thought—full of love and confidence. If you possess such a faith, God (Wisdom) will not withhold His truth from you, but He will reveal His works to you credibly, visibly, and consolingly."

As for imagination, Paracelsus equates it with meditation, a cognitive awareness that receives the messages and translates the revelations that prayer and faith engender. As the mystic Jacob Boehme declared, and as the psychologist Carl Gustav Jung was later to discover (see pages 50–53), alchemy is the language that speaks to the active human imagination.

THE PRINCIPLE ELEMENTS OF ALCHEMY

The inscription around the wheel reads "visit the interior of the earth, rectify it, and you will discover the hidden stone." The Latin acronym spells "vitriol" the alkahest or universal solvent that penetrates all metals.

Although a pious Christian, Paracelsus's concept of the absolute is not the divine intellect of a paternal God, but the *mysterium magnum* ("great mystery"), the source from which all things issue and to which all things return, like the Brahma of Hinduism and the Dao of Chinese mysticism. Native American mysticism shares this concept and also shares with Paracelsus an all-embracing definition of medicine as the language of nature, through which meaning is transmitted to us. Paracelsus's greatest contribution to alchemy lies in the emphasis he put on its medicinal, transformative value, bringing Western alchemy into line with the Chinese and Indian systems. He developed a series of alchemical processes for making medicines, which he called spagyric. We will learn some of these processes in the practical section (see pages 110–123).

ONE OF THE STRANGEST ENIGMAS IN MODERN EUROPEAN HISTORY WAS
THE ROSICRUCIAN PHENOMENON, WHICH MARKED ALCHEMY'S MOST
SIGNIFICANT ROLE IN THE POLITICAL ARENA OF EUROPE

THE ROSICRUCIAN PHENOMENON

Rosicrucianism has its roots in the information explosion generated by the invention of the printing press. It was the printed word that had allowed Martin Luther's repudiation of the Roman Catholic Church, and

Whatsoever is published, and made known to everyone, concerning our Fraternity...let no man esteem lightly of it. CONFESSIO FRATERNITATIS

the events that ensued, to be publicized throughout Europe. Like the Internet today, print allowed religious reformers, alchemists, and Christian cabalists to spread their faiths and come into contact with each other. Common to most of them was the belief that the Catholic Church was suppressing the secret knowledge of the spirit. In 1614, a manifesto entitled *Fama Fraternitatis* ("Declaration of the Brotherhood") was printed in Germany and widely circulated. The authors claimed to represent an illuminated brotherhood of adepts, whose ambition was a "General Reformation of the Whole Wide World." The fraternity was said to have

THE INVISIBLE COLLEGE OF THE ROSICRUCIANS

The college is depicted here as a mobile castle supported by the hand of God and triumphing over its foes. The chymist Robert Boyle referred to "our invisible college" before the establishment of the Royal Society, of which he was a founding member.

been founded by one Christian Rosencreutz, who was born in 1378 and died at the age of one hundred and six. The *Fama Fraternitatis* recounts the life of Brother Rosencreutz ("Rose-cross," when translated from the German), detailing his magical journey to the East; his subsequent fruitless attempts to impart his wisdom to the learned men of Europe; the founding of the secret Brotherhood of the Rosy Cross, whose first rule is "to heal the sick for free"; and his burial in a strange and wonderful tomb.

The *Fama Fraternitatis* tells how this tomb was opened after one-hundred-and-twenty years by later initiates of the brotherhood. Therein they found Brother Rosencreutz's miraculously preserved body, and in his hand a parchment book, at the end of which is a eulogy in which Brother C. R. is described "as a man admitted into the mysteries and secrets of heaven and earth through the divine revelations, subtle cogitations, and unwearied toil of his life." In his journeys through Arabia and Africa he collected a treasure surpassing kings and emperors; but finding it not suitable for his times, he kept it guarded for posterity to uncover, and appointed loyal and faithful heirs of his arts and also of his name. He constructed a microcosm corresponding in all motions to the macrocosm and finally drew up this compendium of things past, present, and to come.

ENGRAVED TITLE FROM DEE'S MONAS HIEROGLYPHICA

The central glyph is a composite of all the symbols of the planets contained within an egg and representing the sum of Creation. This glyph is a key, which through correct application can unlock the mysteries of life.

the fama fraternitatis in ferment

The *Fama Fraternitatis* leads the reader to understand that Christian Rosencreutz was an adept, for the "treasure" that he collected includes the secret of transmutation. Although warning against fraudulent alchemists and berating "gold-makers," the *Fama Fraternitatis* infers that the brotherhood holds the secrets to a genuine alchemical wisdom that boasts "a thousand better things" than the transmutation of metals. It is suggested that in the right hands this wisdom can lead to the transcendental enlightenment not just of individuals, but of the whole of Christendom. The manifesto also invites "some few" to join the brotherhood, without providing any clue as to how this might be achieved.

The *Fama Fraternitatis* caused a furor, and its impact was increased over the next two years with the publication of a further manifesto, known as the *Confessio*, and a strangely compelling alchemical allegory called *The Chemical Wedding of Christian Rosencreutz*. Further publications in France, England, Germany, and Holland led people to believe that Rosicrucian initiates were secretly living among them and carefully selecting worthy personages to join their "Invisible College." No true Rosicrucian was allowed to admit to being such, with the result that nobody claimed to be a Rosicrucian. The affair remained a cause célèbre, with hundreds of publications appearing on the subject, most in the form of replies to the manifestos.

In 1623, placards appeared in Paris, France, announcing the invisible presence in the city of the Brethren of the Rose Cross. These caused equal measures of excitement and alarm. The manifestos had, by this time, been widely read and even more widely discussed. Many hoped that a new enlightenment was about to dawn, as the manifestos promised. Enemies of these ideas, such as the Jesuits, retaliated by producing bogus Rosicrucian manifestos with the aim of portraying the brethren as vicious devil-worshipers. This led to crazed witch-hunts of the kind that the Catholic League was carrying out in the conquered Protestant lands of Bohemia and the Palatine.

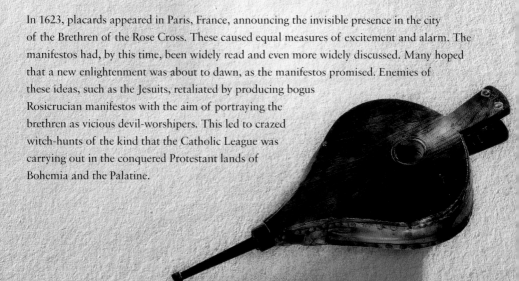

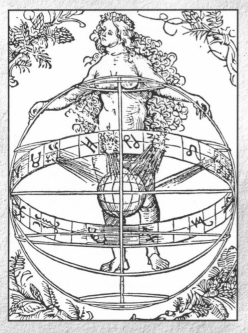

the ROSICRUCIANS

So who were these mysterious Rosicrucians? A German Lutheran called Johan Valentin Andreae was certainly the author of *The Chemical Wedding of Christian Rosencreutz*, later claiming that he wrote it as a "jest." The profound alchemical insight and resonance of the work suggests his claim to be somewhat disingenuous, however. Andreae may have been the author of the manifestos as well, although he always denied it. The manifestos were inspired to some degree by the alchemist Dr. John Dee (d. 1608), the astrologer and mage of Queen Elizabeth I of England, who seems to have had a similar mission as those laid out in the manifestos, that is the "General Reformation of the Whole Wide World,"

and whose *Monas Hieroglyphica* ("Hieroglyphic Monad") is extensively paraphrased, its symbol appearing on the title page of *The Chemical Wedding of Christian Rosencreutz*.

The Polish alchemist Michael Sendivogius probably visited the German university town of Tübingen while Andreae was studying there, and Andreae, who would have heard of Sendivogius's transmutations, would have made every effort to meet the founder of the Society of Unknown Philosophers. The *Fama Fraternitatis* echoes sentiments expressed by the Polish alchemist in the preface of his *Treatise on Sulfur*, while the *Confessio* quotes from his *Twelve Treatises*. Sendivogius was a model Rosicrucian in many ways: widely traveled, extremely well connected, and a prophetic Utopian reformer; a Paracelsian physician who had effected famous cures using his own alchemical medicines; the publisher of several important alchemical texts anonymously (that is, not dedicated to princes or kings); and a man who appears to have been of high moral character.

Another profound influence on the manifestos was a prophetic–apocalyptic work by Simon Studion called *Naometria* (1604), which reveals hopes for a hermetically inspired Protestant League between Henri IV of France (first a Huguenot Protestant, later a Catholic), King James I of England, and Frederick I, Duke of Württemberg. The assassination of Henri IV, however, meant that Rosicrucian hopes were shifted on to the inexperienced Frederick V, Elector Palatine of the Rhine, and son-in-law of James I of England. These hopes were dashed by Frederick's disastrous defeat by the Hapsburg Catholics at the Battle of the White Mountain in Bohemia in 1620, which presaged the Thirty Years War (fought between Catholics and Protestants).

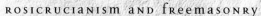

ROSICRUCIANISM AND FREEMASONRY

It is possible that Andreae and his coauthors, if he had any, were influenced by Freemasonry, the earliest-known statutes of which date back to 1598 and 1599. The reverse is certainly true. The second-known reference to the "Mason's word" appears in the freemason Henry Adamson's *The Muses Threnodie* (1638):

> *For what we do pressage is not in grosse*
> *For we be brethren of the Rosie Cross:*
> *We have the Mason's word and second sight,*
> *Things for to come we can foretell aright.*

Freemasonry, the most famous and influential of all secret societies, absorbed the ideals and mysticism of Rosicrucianism, providing it with a lasting, though sadly as yet unfulfilled, legacy.

ROSICRUCIAN INFLUENCES

Although Christian Rosencreutz appears to be an allegorical figure, there is no doubt that many significant and gifted people were immediately inspired to espouse the beliefs of his purported followers. Chief

*This depiction of the Rose
Cross is taken from* Summum
bonum, *by Robert Fludd, 1629.
Fludd was a Paracelsian physician
and alchemist. He considered
himself a Rosicrucian, though
he never claimed to have
been in contact with them.*

among these were the Englishman
Robert Fludd and the German
Michael Maier, both Paracelsian
physicians. Fludd produced a
series of brilliantly illustrated
works elucidating the philosophy
of microcosm and macrocosm, while Maier, formerly personal physician to the Holy Roman
Emperor Rudolph II, produced some of the most beautiful and profound works emphasizing the
spiritual aspect of alchemy.

Real Rosicrucian societies did come into being, a significant early one being the *Gold-und
Rosenkreutzer* ("Brotherhood of the Gold and Rosy Cross,") which came into being in
Germany), and under which name several notable alchemical texts were published, mostly of
an allegorical and spiritual nature. Today there are Rosicrucian societies with lodges all over
the world that claim a direct link to the original source.

Behind the whole Rosicrucian phenomenon looms the figure of
Paracelsus, who is the only contemporaneous figure to be
singled out for praise in the *Fama Fraternitatis*. His frustrations
in the face of the "learned and 'wise-seeming' men" strike a
familiar note and underline the resistance that the establishment
has always had to sacred magic. The Rosicrucians sought to
put in place a new magical religious and political
establishment. Its time has yet to come.

HERALD ANGELS AWAKEN A SLUMBERING ALCHEMIST WITH TRUMPET BLASTS

Would we but wake up and perceive the truth we would see a stairway to heaven before us with guides willing to help us ascend.

DEW, THE DISTILLED ESSENCE OF HEAVEN ABOVE AND EARTH BELOW,
IS A CONDENSATION OF THE UNIVERSAL SPIRIT OR SECRET FIRE,
KNOWN IN INDIA AS *PRANA* AND IN CHINA AS *QI*.

THE DISTILLATION OF DEW, THE ELIXIR OF LIFE

Drawn up as moisture by the action of the sun, and condensed by the cool of the night to settle again on the earth, no other substance in nature more perfectly reflects the central alchemical process of circulation than dew. To the Druids it was the most sacred form of water; to the Ancient Chinese it symbolized immortality, while in the cabala it represents resurrection.

I am the moisture which preserves everything in nature and makes it live,
I pass from the upper to the lower planes;
I am the heavenly dew and the fat of the land;
I am the fiery water and the watery fire; nothing may live without me...
FROM AN 18TH-CENTURY ROSICRUCIAN TEXT

Many important alchemical elixirs and processes utilize dew, including the "Wet Path" of the Philosopher's Stone. Dew features as the *prima materia* in one of the most famous alchemical books, the *Mutus Liber* ("Mute Book"), first published in 1677. Almost entirely wordless (hence the title), the book consists of fifteen engravings depicting a sequence of alchemical processes performed by a man and a woman, and it remains highly influential in modern alchemical practice.

We could make Angel Water with a distillation train, but there are ways of obtaining dew that do not require an alchemical laboratory or expensive equipment. The illustration from the Mute Book shows exactly how to proceed. Cloths

COLLECTING THE DEW

The alchemist and his soror mystica ("mystic sister") capture the dew by wringing out wet towels into a basin.

stretched over posts gather the dew, while from the heavens above stream rays of etheric forces, rich with the quickening spirit of life. This is the Secret Fire that impregnates the dew, and the ram and the bull, representing the zodiac signs of Aries and Taurus, indicate that it flows most strongly in the northern hemisphere's springtime, from the end of March to the end of May.

Dew is collected using clean, cotton or linen sheets or towels stretched tightly across pegs a little way off the ground: this is important, as the etheric forces in the dew will be drained if the cloth sags and touches the earth. May-dew is considered the most potent, preferably collected on clear nights leading up to the full moon. At dawn, before sunrise, detach the cloths carefully from the pegs and wring them out into a large glass or earthenware basin. Filter the dew (use unbleached coffee filters) into a glass jar, seal tightly, and set in the sun till noon. Strain off into another glass jar. The dew is now ready to drink.

CHAPTER II
ALCHEMY RESTORED

*T*he seventeenth century marked both the greatest flowering of alchemy and also its decline. The so-called "Enlightenment" fostered humanist, rational, and materialist notions of the world, which were supported by the emergence of modern science, ironically on the back of the alchemists' work. Science provided more and more useful applications that seemed to make life easier and more efficient. No longer attracting the greatest minds, and increasingly marginalized, alchemy went underground, and it was not until the nineteenth century that a strong occult revival began in reaction to scientific reductionism. The discovery of radioactivity showed that the theory of transmutation, so long denied by science, was not, after all, fundamentally in error. With each discovery of quantum physics, alchemy stood further redeemed, or was, at least, theoretically arguable. Physics has now acquired some of the attributes of the intuitive arts. Science has proved that everything is possible, even alchemy. In recent decades, developments in understanding have led to a wholesale re-evaluation of alchemy, as we shall see in the pages that follow.

behold the mighty secrets
and wonders before you

MICROCOSM AND MACROCOSM

The alchemist as master of the polarities reflected in the Microcosm, which itself reflects the Macrocosm. The extraordinary richness of symbolism in this engraving rewards many hours of contemplation.

ALTHOUGH MOST PRACTICAL ALCHEMISTS QUESTION HIS UNDERSTANDING OF THE DYNAMICS OF ALCHEMY, THE PSYCHOLOGIST C. G. JUNG'S CONTRIBUTION TO THE RE-EVALUATION OF ALCHEMY AS A HIGHLY SOPHISTICATED SCIENCE OF THE SOUL HAS PROVED VERY INFLUENTIAL

alchemy and psychology

From the late eighteenth to the early twentieth centuries, the investigation of alchemy was confined to occultists and historians of science. During the early 1920s, the Swiss psychologist Carl Gustav Jung started studying alchemy when he realized that many of its key symbols were surfacing in the dreams of his patients. His own nervous breakdown a few years earlier had already made him aware of a mythical realm of what he called *archetypes*—powerful images arising from the "universal unconscious" shared by all humans. His studies and lectures on alchemical symbolism were collated in his book *Psychology and Alchemy*. Richly illustrated with a great number of previously unpublished alchemical images, it was published in 1944 and has remained in print ever since. Its influence was considerable, and it

almost single-handedly presented alchemy as a subject worthy of profound investigation. Jung established that the body of alchemical works presents an astonishing consistency and complexity of ideas and images, in spite of its apparently riddling and often contradictory language. This, he contends, can be no accident: "A symbolism as rich as that of alchemy invariably owes its existence to some adequate cause, never to mere whim or play of fancy." The alchemists, he realized, were neither deluding, nor simply amusing, themselves: they were onto something of enormous significance.

THE TRIPLE-CROWNED MAGISTERY

The Secret Fire liberated from the Four Elements travels up the coils of the serpents and, descending via their tongues, exalts the elixir contained in the vessel.

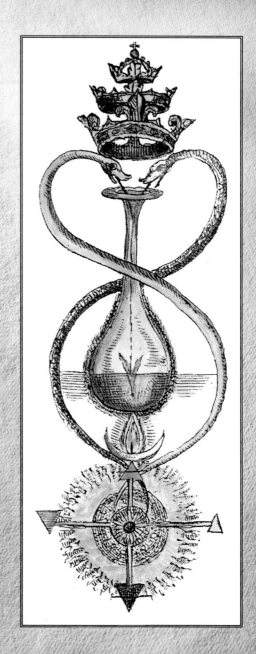

existential alchemy

Jung's study of alchemy inspired his concept of *individuation*—a person's liberation from his or her own psychic labyrinth and the resolution of the personal psychodrama. His work with Austrian psychiatrist Sigmund Freud on sexual psychology gave him insights into the erotic aspect of alchemy, the Chemical Wedding, with its emphasis on the union of opposites. While many alchemists and mystics reproach Jung for confining alchemy to purely psychological models, it is fair to say that he recognized that alchemy is concerned not just with the resolution or redemption of humanity alone, but also of nature itself. His main interest lay in how the psyche responds to the riddle of existence rather than in the nature and purpose of Creation. Jung's subject is the psychology of humanity, not life. The alchemist's subject is life itself and his or her relationship with it; the intense and intimate study of which reveals the alchemist and life to be the same thing, the all. In this respect, Jung's view of alchemy is limited to a psychological viewpoint, although the contemporary alchemist Professor Manfred Junius (see page 60) has heard on good authority that in the latter years of his life Jung set up a laboratory for practical work.

Jung's other major books on alchemy are *Alchemical Studies* and the monumental *Mysterium Coniunctionis* ("Mystery of Union"), which explores the nature of

opposites, particularly the polarity of male and female as represented in alchemy by the Sun and the Moon, and the Red King and the White Queen. He also elucidates the understanding that the world is a reflection of the inner psyche, that in a very real sense each individual is responsible for everything that happens in the outside world. This is the key to understanding the true significance of humanity as a microcosm; as above, so below; as within, so without.

EPIGRAM 34 OF MICHAEL MAIER'S ATALANTA FUGIENS, *1618*

"Resplendent glows the bath when he's conceived, and sky when he is born; then red he strides across the waters, whitens on the mountains, he whom the learned make their only care. A stone he is yet not; a gift from Heaven, which given by God to you, will make you blest."

IN 1926, THE FRENCH ALCHEMIST FULCANELLI, WHOSE REAL IDENTITY IS UNKNOWN, PRODUCED, IN HIS MASTERPIECE, *THE MYSTERY OF THE CATHEDRALS*, A TOUR OF THE ESOTERIC TRADITION IN THE WEST AS DISPLAYED ON THE WALLS OF GOTHIC CATHEDRALS

The Fulcanelli Phenomenon

During the 1920s, an unusual book appeared in Paris called *The Mystery of the Cathedrals*, written under the alchemical pseudonym Fulcanelli. This book elaborated with great authority the idea that the Gothic cathedrals of Europe were nothing less than alchemical texts written in stone, containing within their architecture all of the symbols of the Great Work. As the distinguished scholar Walter Lang wrote in the introduction to the English edition of *The Mystery of the Cathedrals:* "It has long been believed that the Gothic cathedrals were secret textbooks of some hidden knowledge; that behind the gargoyles and the glyphs, the rose windows and the flying buttresses, a mighty secret lay, all but openly displayed. This is no longer a theory."

Fulcanelli suggests that esoteric Hermetic philosophy was the impulse behind the astonishingly sudden flourishing of Gothic architecture in medieval Europe. Not only did Gothic architecture display extraordinary technical advances on the preceding Romanesque style, but it was executed on a vast scale. Between 1170 and 1270, the building of some eighty cathedrals and five hundred churches of near-cathedral size was begun in France alone. The same impulse inspired the legends of the Holy Grail that were also written during this period, a time of troubadours and poets of courtly love who heralded the age of chivalry and the institution of mystical knightly orders like the Order of the Garter in England.

MULTIPLE SYMBOLISM

This emblem combines alchemical, Rosicrucian, and Masonic symbolism. The conjoined serpents represent the Solve et Coagula, *the rotation of the fixed and the volatile. At the center of the Seal of Solomon is the mystic rose, framed by a set square, dividers, and ruler, all symbols of Freemasonry.*

Where did this impulse come from? Probably from the Holy Land. The First Crusade and the establishment of the Kingdom of Jerusalem at the beginning of the twelfth century brought Europeans into direct contact with Islam. The Knights Templar, an order founded to protect the pilgrimage routes through the Holy Land, always had links with sources of secret knowledge, and it is probable that some of their ranks were initiated into Sufism. This mystical current of Islam had embraced a profound understanding of hermetism, Neo-Platonism, and alchemy since at least the time of Jabir. Sacred geometry and erotic religious symbolism were also part of the Sufi mix, and some of these elements started to enter Europe during the twelfth century.

Fulcanelli also elaborated at length on the phonetic cabala, a system of puns and wordplay used by adepts both to conceal and reveal esoteric meaning. This form of cant or argot (hence *l'art Gothique*—"Gothic art"), also known as the "language of the birds," is a crucial key to deciphering alchemical treatises and symbolism and to reading nature's signs.

ENCOUNTER WITH FULCANELLI

Fulcanelli remains one of the most enigmatic and mysterious occult figures of the twentieth century. He rediscovered the long-lost alchemical process that produced the famous blue-and-red stained glass of such cathedrals as Chartres, in France, and is said to have performed a transmutation in front of reliable witnesses before disappearing during the 1930s. In *The Morning of the Magicians* (1963), Jacques Bergier describes receiving an unexpected visit in 1937 from a stranger whom he believed to be Fulcanelli. At the time Bergier was engaged in nuclear research with the noted scientist Andre Helbronner. Bergier asked his visitor to explain the nature of his work and received this reply: "You are asking me to summarize in four minutes four thousand years of philosophy and my whole life's work. Furthermore you are asking me to translate

into plain words concepts for which such a language is not intended. All the same, I can say this: you will not be unaware that in present-day official science the part played by the observer becomes more and more important. Relativity, the principle of indeterminacy, demonstrates the extent to which the observer today intervenes in all these phenomena. The secret of alchemy is this: there is a way of manipulating what modern science calls a force-field. This force-field acts upon the observer and puts him in a privileged position in relation to the universe. From this privileged position, he has access to the realities which are normally concealed from us by time and space, matter and energy. This is what we call the Great Work."

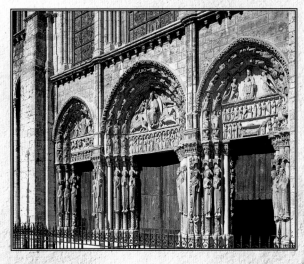

NOTRE-DAME DE PARIS
Fulcanelli believed this cathedral to be a
Hermetic masterwork written in stone.
In The Mystery of the Cathedrals *he*
describes in detail the alchemical
symbolism of many of its stone carvings.

"But what about the Philosopher's Stone? The making of gold?" Bergier asked. "Those are only applications of it, particular cases. The vital thing is not the transmutation of metals, but that of the experimenter himself. It is an ancient secret that a few people rediscover each century." Bergier was impressed by the stranger's knowledge of nuclear energy, which surpassed his own and proved highly prescient. He was warned of the appalling dangers involved in nuclear fission. After the war Bergier, who had worked in Intelligence, was debriefed by the forerunner of the CIA. His testimony pursuaded the authorities to try and track Fulcanelli down. They never found him. The only person who claims to have seen Fulcanelli since Bergier is his former pupil Eugene Canseliet. Summoned by his master to a castle in the mountains of Spain in 1952, Canseliet described his master as appearing twenty years younger than he had twenty years earlier.

ALCHEMY SLIPPED QUIETLY BENEATH THE SURFACE FOR MOST OF THE EIGHTEENTH AND
NINETEENTH CENTURIES, BUT IT NEVER DIED OUT. IN GERMANY, PARTICULARLY,
PARACELSIAN PHYSICIANS CONTINUED TO PREPARE AND ADMINISTER ALCHEMICAL
MEDICINES, WHILE KEEPING THEIR ART TO THEMSELVES. IN THE TWENTIETH CENTURY,
ALCHEMY ONCE MORE RAISED ITS HEAD ABOVE THE PARAPET

The Modern Alchemical Tradition

During the course of the twentieth century, alchemy experienced a revival that would have been
unimaginable during the nineteenth. We have already looked at the role played by Carl Gustav
Jung in this renaissance, but there have been other significant contributors in different fields, too.

From the 1920s to the 1940s, Dr. Lili Kolisko, a colleague of the Austrian philosopher and
mystic Rudolf Steiner, undertook a series of experiments to validate Steiner's theories
regarding subtle forces at work within plants and soil. She then used a form of
chromatography called capillary dynamolisis, which validated the alchemists' ancient
association of the seven classical planets with their corresponding metals—for example, the
Sun and gold, the Moon and silver, and so on. These experiments were successfully repeated
by others, including the English researcher Nick Kolleström.

In 1962, the French scientist Louis Kervran published a book called
Biological Transmutations, which described a series of experiments
showing that the low-energy transmutation of certain elements is a
biological reality in both plants and animals, including humans.
Physicists were, of course, highly skeptical, but Kervran's work was
subsequently confirmed by Japanese, French, and Swiss scientists.
During the 1990s, Oliver Costa de Beauregard, Professor of
Theoretical Physics at the Institut de Physique Théorique, Henri
Poincaré (Faculty of Sciences, University of Paris), evolved a
theory that places these discoveries within the framework of
modern physics.

FRONTISPIECE TO THE APHORISMS
OF BARON URIBEGRUS, 1690

Duke Frederick of Saxe-Gotha is said to have successfully tested the method for producing the Stone illustrated here. A small medal was struck from the alchemical gold in commemoration.

Adam McLean sums up the implications of Kervran and de Beauregard's work thus: "We see that in living matter there not only occurs the chemical reactions (electromagnetic forces) of photosynthesis involving the absorption of photons of light from the sun, but also weak interactions that can effect the nuclear structure of matter, activated through the participation of cosmic energy in the form of neutrinos that stream down upon the earth from the depths of the universe. A full awareness of the consequences of these ideas should have a profound influence upon many domains of modern science, not least in agriculture, dietetics, and healing…Thus with Louis Kervran's profoundly important work we could stand upon the threshold of a turning point in the physical sciences, and we seem to have the meeting ground between contemporary physics and an esoteric science of the ethers. One can only hope that such research is fully followed up and the profound implications for the present rigid view of the mechanism of living matter are not missed."

modern alchemical practice

Concurrent with scientific validations of alchemical theories has been a
resurgence of practical medicinal alchemy, based in particular on the teachings
of Paracelsus. The most significant figure behind this fresh impetus was the
Austrian alchemist Albert Riedel, known as Frater Albertus. After attending
a series of alchemy lessons provided by AMORC, the California-based
Rosicrucian society, in 1960 he published *The Alchemist's
Handbook*, providing straightforward instructions
for the production of Paracelsian plant elixirs
made with modern laboratory apparatus. Frater
Albertus founded the Paracelsus Research Society in
Salt Lake City, Utah, teaching alchemy to students at a
very low cost and producing a quarterly magazine from
1960 to 1972. Frater Albertus made contact with other
practicing alchemists and gave hundreds of people,
including many of today's best teachers, their first real
introduction to alchemy. He emphasized the spiritual and
medicinal virtues of alchemy.

Following Frater Albertus's death in 1984, former students of his who were looking for another
teacher contacted Jean Dubuis, a French alchemist and nuclear scientist who ran an organization
called Les Philosophes de la Nature, which provided courses in herbal spagyrics along the same
lines as the principles taught by Frater Albertus and mineral alchemy. Dubuis donated the
text of his lessons to the American students, who had it translated into English and formed an
organization called the Philosophers of Nature. The group is less active at the moment, but still
provides courses and seminar videos.

One of the most widely respected contemporary alchemists is Professor Manfred Junius, who
was born in Germany in 1929. He spent thirty-five years in India practicing Ayurvedic medicine
and studying Indian alchemy, which emphasizes medicinal work. Upon his return to Europe
during the 1970s, Junius studied Western alchemy with the Italian Augusto Pancaldi, who soon
encouraged him to attempt the *circulatum minus*, a notoriously difficult plant work that had
not been perfected since Baron Urbigerus published his treatise on the subject in 1690. Although
he was unconvinced of his readiness, Junius was nevertheless persuaded and achieved success,
producing a clear, colorless liquid with certain remarkable qualities that defy scientific
explanation. In a matter of minutes, it separates out the soluble properties of fresh plant

EX MORTE VEST...

...IVUAMEN

THE UNIVERSAL MEDICINE

The Universal Medicine, or Philosophers' Stone, exemplified as the sum of the virtues of the planets, is here personified as a crowned sun shining on the figure of Hermes.

matter without dissolving them into itself, despite the fact that it consists predominantly of plant alcohol. With Junius's help, a further six individuals have since achieved the same success. Junius's book, *The Practical Handbook of Plant Alchemy*, is a modern classic that is recommended to anyone who wishes to explore laboratory alchemy as the best place to start. Junius runs an Ayurvedic practice in South Australia and a commercial laboratory, Australerba, which produces spagyric medicines, herbal honeys, and tonics. He teaches in Germany and Switzerland every summer.

In Germany, where alchemy survived more continuously than elsewhere, there is an alchemy association with about one-hundred-and-twenty members, a good number of whom hold practical workshops on a fairly regular basis. In Germany, too, are several commercial laboratories that have been selling spagyric remedies for as long as eighty years.

WORK

The *Great Work*, or *Opus Magnum*, is the term used by alchemists to describe the conscious effort to achieve the highest state of purity. The term is applied both to the Outer Work, the perfection of the Philosopher's Stone, and to the Inner Work, the achievement of divine consciousness. In order to proceed along this path, the initiate must understand, intellectually at first, the nature of cosmic reality. The Great Work also refers to Creation itself. Creation materializes to the point where it produces a godless ego that believes in nothing but itself. Such a point of extreme selfishness creates a spiritual vacuum. Nature abhors a vacuum, and thus the ego pulls the full weight of the universe down upon its head. Shocked by the full awareness of its mortality and impotence, the ego experiences the initiation of the nadir, the big wake-up call. Humbled, the initiate starts to seek divinity as his or her salvation and begins the path of return. Just as the microcosm is the mirror image of the macrocosm, so the Great Work of the initiate is the process of the Great Work of Creation in reverse. How does this work? Let us start at the beginning, with the A, B, C, the 1, 2, 3, of Creation.

ELEMENTS OF THE GREAT WORK

Note the shield in the top panel displaying the three primary colors of the Work and a yin-yang-type device. The pillars are labeled Nature and Art.

ONE PLUS NAUGHT MAKES TEN

Hermetic numerology can only hint at the why of Creation, but it can give us a profound insight into the what and how. This is sacred numerology that differs from mathematics in many fundamental ways: it perceives numbers as qualities rather than quantities; there are no fractions; one divided by two equals two; naught proceeds from one; one plus naught equals three. Number divines the divine.

The mystery of creation can never be revealed in ordinary words, but wordplay and symbols can spark intuitive understanding. This is the phonetic cabala, the "language of the birds," the mystical *Langue Verte* ("Green Language"), true gibberish. Let us play.

the one

In the beginning, there was one: the absolute, the all in one, the one in all. This one is the "I" of God, represented by a rod or, in alchemy, a serpent. It is the absolute symbol of masculinity. It is God the Father, the active, engendering principle. But what can one do on one's own? How can there be masculinity when there is, as yet, no femininity? What came first, the cock or the egg? Alchemy answers this riddle with another: the figure of the ouroboros, the serpent with its tail in its mouth. This is potentially both male and female, both "I" and "O." It is the beginning and the end of the Great Work. It is all and nothing. It is male and female, but also neither.

from one to zero

In order for one to multiply, it must sacrifice its undivided unity. By turning on itself through meditation, "I" becomes "O." Because zero proceeds from one as one's first consequence, zero should therefore not be considered nothing: it is a naught, a figure with no defined quantity, but a figure nevertheless. As a symbol, "O" represents the passive receptive principle: the open vagina (hole); the sum and matrix of all possibilities (whole); the (unfertilized) egg; the eternal feminine; and God the Mother.

the Logos

This supreme sacrifice of self-contained, undifferentiated unity is symbolized by the beheading of the king: "I" becomes "i," thereby making the point. The point is the *logos*, the word; the seed that fertilizes the egg.

Let there be Light

The cosmic marriage has taken place. The egg has been fertilized and, after a count of nine, gives birth to the Sun, the eye of God, represented by an "O" with a point in the middle, the symbol of gold. The number of the Sun is ten, symbolizing the cosmos, the paradigms of creation, completion, and perfection. It is the number of fingers that come together in prayer. In Roman and Chinese numerals, ten is represented by a cross ("x"). Graphically, "IO" is an archetypal symbol for marriage.

THE EYE OF GOD

The separation is taking place as the One sacrifices Unity in order to fertilize the cosmic egg. This image is taken from a series of illustrations that depict a Hermetic understanding of the stages of Creation.

IN THE BEGINNING, THERE WAS THE ONE; THE ABSOLUTE, THE ALL IN ONE, THE ONE IN
ALL. THE CREATIVE PRINCIPLE THAT GIVES RISE TO DIVERSITY IS THE GREAT MYSTERY,
THE INDESTRUCTIBLE ABSOLUTE CONSCIOUSNESS OF THE UNIVERSE. ALCHEMY SEEKS TO
FIND THIS DIVINE PRINCIPLE CONCEALED WITHIN ALL THINGS AND RESURRECT IT

THE DIVINE PRINCIPLE

Prima materia, the "first matter," is the divine principle, the absolute, the goal of the alchemist, the one thing that he or she wants to find, to perfect, to become. It represents the greatest riddle and secret of alchemy. It is both the beginning and the end of the Great Work, hence it is symbolized by the ouroboros, among other things. It must be identified in its raw, debased state, within and without, and brought to perfection "gently and with great ingenuity" (*The Emerald Tablet*).

What is it? What is the "matter"? I don't know. No alchemist will ever tell you, for it cannot be told. Only you can know what's really the matter. Although we all have it in common, it's your story. We can say that it is the primary stuff of the world, the nitty-gritty, the rub, the salt of the earth. But it is also ethereal and intangible. It is particle and wave, matter and energy. According to *Gloria Mundi* ("Glory of the World"), 1526, "it is familiar to all men, both young and old, is found in the country, in the village, in the town, in all things created by God; yet it is despised by all. Rich and poor handle it every day. It is cast into the street by servant maids. Children play with it. Yet no one prizes it, though, next to the human soul, it is the most beautiful and the most precious thing upon earth and has the power to pull down kings and princes. Nevertheless, it is esteemed the vilest and meanest of earthly things."

Without identifying this thing, the Great Work cannot be begun. The *Sophic Hydrolith* ("Waterstone of the Wise" 1619) tells us, "This Matter is found in one thing, out of which alone our Stone is prepared… It is found potentially everywhere, and

THE CRUX OF THE MATTER

In order for One to multiply, it must sacrifice its undivided unity. Thus all that issue from the One may participate in Being. The cross is shaped like the Tau, the last letter of the Hebrew alphabet, suggesting completion. The beginning is the end. We too may be resurrected from the cross of matter by sacrificing our separate individuality.

in everything, but in all its perfection and fullness only in one thing." Everything has been tried. The puffers tried "poudres diverse, asshes, dong, pisse and cley," as Chaucer's Canon Yeoman tells us, without success. But everyone who really seeks it with all of his or her heart and soul will find it.

THE ARISING OF DIVERSITY OUT OF UNITY IS THE SUBJECT OF HERMETIC NUMEROLOGY, HENCE MARIA PROHETISSA'S LEGENDARY MAXIM "ONE BECOMES TWO, TWO BECOMES THREE, AND OUT OF THE THIRD COMES THE ONE AS THE FOURTH"

Duality

In the first book of the *Hermetica*, Hermes relates a vision of the Creation: "I beheld a boundless view; all was changed into light, a mild and joyous light; and I marveled when I saw it. And in a little while, there had come to be in one part a downward-tending darkness, terrible and grim…And thereafter I saw the darkness changing into a watery substance, which was unspeakably tossed about, and gave forth smoke as from a fire; and I heard it making an indescribable sound of lamentation; for there was sent forth from it an inarticulate cry." This is the rending of the One, the wrenching pain of separation as the Absolute falls in upon itself to precipitate the process leading to manifestation.

IN THE BED OF LOVE

The Queen (Mercury) encourages the King (Sulfur) to let his spirit fly. It is desire that draws the polarized opposites together in harmony. Thus two signifies both separation and desire.

The divine principle separates into two to form the matrix, the womb of creation from which all things issue. Two is duality, the law of opposites, the dynamic tension of the created universe. It is light and dark, active and passive, high and low, male and female, yin and yang. It represents desire because all things born in duality seek their mate, their other half. These couples are represented alchemically by sulfur and mercury, the Red King and the White Queen, the Sun and the Moon. As lovers who seek union, they represent balance and harmony. These are complementary pairs, but two also represents separation.

The philosopher must deal with this inner turbulence and reconcile the antagonistic opposites, such as love and hate, within him- or herself in order to find transcendence in the one. The internal conflict is sometimes portrayed in alchemical emblems by pairs of fighting creatures like dogs and wolves, dragons and birds. These creatures often represent specific substances that are used to separate the pure from the impure, the subtle from the gross. For the *prima materia* itself is trapped in the dualistic world and must be freed from its prison in order to be perfected. This principle is represented by two dragons biting each other's tails. One is winged (volatile), the other is wingless (fixed). The old motto of alchemy *Solve et Coagula* ("dissolve [the body] and bind [the spirit]") must be applied (see pages 32–33). With patient repetition of this process, the fixed (matter) and the volatile (spirit) become perfected as one. The perfected matter or adept is often symbolized by the androgyne or hermaphrodite.

SUN AND MOON
"The Sun needs the Moon as the cock needs the hen." So suggests coquettish Luna to reluctant Sol, pointing to the strutting cock.

THE UNION OF SULFUR (SOUL) AND MERCURY
(SPIRIT), THE OPPOSITES CREATED BY DUALITY,
ENGENDERS SALT (FORM), WHICH IS THE THIRD
PRINCIPLE. ALL THINGS MANIFESTED IN CREATION,
THEREFORE, CONSIST OF SOUL, SPIRIT, AND FORM

THE TRINITY

As we have seen, the act of
creation forms a trinity of
God the Mother, God the
Father, and God the Sun. These three aspects of the
absolute are analogous to soul, spirit, and body, called
in alchemy sulfur, mercury, and salt. These are
philosophical principles and should not be confused with
the substances of the same name, with which they have
only a very partial connection. These three principles are
present in everything manifested in the universe. Indeed, without any
one of these principles nothing could be. Even minerals. Even elements. It was Paracelsus,
the great reformer of alchemy, who, like Rhazes centuries before him, emphasized the
importance of the third principle of salt in addition to the traditional duad
of sulfur and mercury. Salt adds the third dimension that allows things to
manifest on the material plane. It is the vehicle of physical existence.

SULFUR–is the active, masculine, fiery, solar principle. It is the soul,
consciousness, the individual spirit.

MERCURY–is the passive, feminine, watery, lunar principle. It is
the spirit, the life force, the universal soul in all things.

SALT–is the body, the precipitate, the child of the marriage of
sulfur and mercury, the son of the Sun and the Moon. It mediates
between the two, balancing them, reconciling their opposing

principles, and rendering them complementary and compatible. It is their raison d'être, without which duality would serve no purpose. Duality is established to give birth to Creation, so salt is the child of sulfur and mercury. Like salt, sulfur, the conscious soul, mediates between the body and the spirit, harmonizing and blending them, transforming them into a single essence, which in turn liberates the soul, allowing it to realize its full potential and rendering it immortal.

In its polarity with sulfur, mercury is bound, defined, and specified. But in itself it is mysterious, elusive, ambivalent, and androgynous (only when qualified in relation to sulfur is it fixed as the feminine). It is anonymous, yet has many names: Hyle, Chaos, Chaotic Water, Living Water, Eternal Fountain, Philosophical Basilisk, and even *prima materia*, Original Mercury. When fixed by sulfur, mercury becomes the Great Mother, the principle of life, the vitalizing life force, *Prana, Chi*. Mercury also mediates between sulfur and salt. As Bernard of Treviso explains: "This [Mercury] invades and penetrates, as spirit, the other two principles, salt and sulfur, which it unites and controls constantly, by natural heat." Thus these three philosophical principles express the dynamic that allows the universe—and all things—to be and that explains why Hermes is designated "Thrice Greatest," for he has mastered the triple mystery of creation.

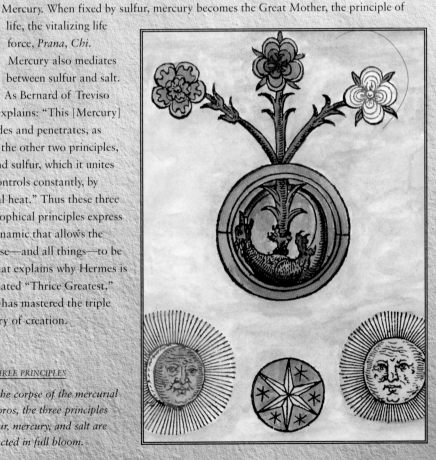

THE THREE PRINCIPLES

From the corpse of the mercurial ouroboros, the three principles of sulfur, mercury, and salt are resurrected in full bloom.

ALL MATERIAL THINGS ARE MIXTURES OF THE FOUR PHILOSOPHICAL ELEMENTS. THE
BALANCE OF THE ELEMENTS DETERMINES THE NATURES OF THINGS. THE DIFFERENCE
BETWEEN ALCOHOL AND WATER, FROM AN ALCHEMICAL PERSPECTIVE, IS THAT ALCOHOL
CONTAINS MORE FIRE AND IS THEREFORE MORE VOLATILE. HENCE IT IS CALLED A SPIRIT

 THE FOUR ELEMENTS

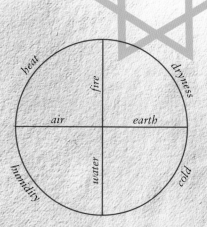

All things have their being in the three
philosophical principles of soul, spirit, and body.
This trinity animates all things in the material
world. The trinity gives rise to the quaternity, the
four philosophical elements of fire, water, earth,
and air, which define the material form of all
manifest things. These elements should not be
confused with the substances with which they
share their names, nor do they correspond to
the chemical elements. Like the trinity, they are
not things, but *principles*. These principles
consist of pairings of four *qualities*: hot, dry,
cold, and moist.

Each element shares both of its qualities with
another element. This provides the dynamic
that allows for transformation within matter.
Earthy solids can melt into watery liquids,
which in turn can become gases, both
flammable and inert, which can condense back
into fluid or burn. Fire is the most volatile of
the elements, earth the most fixed. Fire and air
are the masculine elements, earth and water the
feminine ones. All things are mixta, mixtures of
the four elemental qualities.

 fire—is hot and dry. It is symbolized
by the upward-pointing triangle,
being volatile and ascending.

 air—is hot and moist. Putting a
brake on the ascending nature of
fire, its triangle is crossed.

 water—is cold and moist. As the
descending element, its sign is the
downward-pointing triangle.

 earth—is cold and dry. It halts
the fall of water, hence its triangle
is crossed.

The elements have nothing to do with density. Water (H_2O) and alcohol have a similar density, but alcohol (also known as firewater) contains considerably more elemental fire, while water has more air. Indeed, distilled alcohol, which was first produced by alchemists, was considered a marvelous substance because it seemed to marry the elements of fire and water, while containing the smallest amounts of earth and air.

When Robert Boyle famously debunked the philosophical theory of the elements in the *Sceptical Chymist* (1661), beginning the scientific redefinition of the elements as immutable substances, he was stating what, to the adept, was obvious, but was missing the point. The relevance of the philosophical elements as a key to understanding the dynamics of life remains undimmed.

THE SALAMANDER

The Salamander of mythology is said to live in fire. It is an Elemental creature, a spiritual entity which personifies fire. It is also equated with sulfur, the fiery, solar principle of the duad of sulfur and mercury.

THE QUINTESSENCE

OF ALL THE PHILOSOPHICAL PRINCIPLES, NONE IS AS MYSTERIOUS AND INTANGIBLE AS THE QUINTESSENCE, THE FIFTH ESSENCE OR ELEMENT, WHICH IS CONCEALED WITHIN THE FOUR PHILOSOPHICAL ELEMENTS AND EQUATES WITH THE SECRET FIRE, THE SPARK OF DIVINITY WITHIN ALL THINGS

The four elements conceal within them a fifth element, known as the *quinta essencia*, the quintessence, or Azoth. This has the connotation of being the absolute essence of a thing and, as such, many alchemical magisteries (products or medicines) are called quintessences, particularly those that have been distilled, because distillation releases the soul and spirit from matter. Some alchemists call the spirit of wine (distilled brandy) a quintessence, and, indeed, it fulfills the criteria described by Isaac Newton: "Quintessence is a thing that is spiritual, penetrating, tinging, and incorruptible, which emerges anew from the four elements when they are bound to each other."

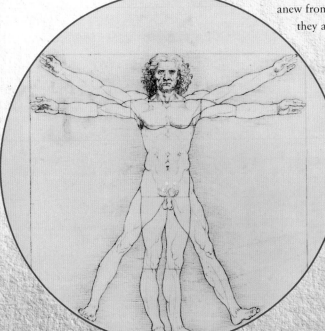

UNIVERSAL MAN

Leonardo da Vinci's famous depiction of magically proportioned Man, who squares the circle and proves himself the ideal Microcosm, the perfect reflection of God, the divine Macrocosm.

Paracelsus considers it to be the extract of the elements, their incorruptible, eternal substratum. Manfred Junius calls it "The origin and goal of all things."

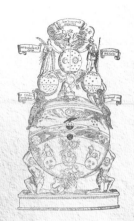

It is often said that the quintessence is not a product of the elements, but one of the three philosophical principles. In fact, it is all three: the trinity in everything. The quintessence is the soul and spirit within all things. It is also the salt that allows it to emerge through the four elements. This reveals it to be nothing less than the secret fire, the spark of eternal light from the first combustion of creation. It is the divinity in all things, the inner sun in which all things find their true identity. Alchemists give it many names: Universal Spirit, Never-failing Source, *clavis philosophorum*, *seminarium mundi*, *substantia coelestis* ("key of the philosophers, nursery of the world, heavenly substance"), Mother of the Waters and, even, Mercurius.

The quintessence can be symbolized by the pentagram, the figure that most perfectly divides the circle. It represents the microcosm, the individual containing the whole universe within itself.

ACCORDING TO LEGEND, THE SEAL OF SOLOMON
WAS A SIGIL SET IN A RING BROUGHT TO SOLOMON
BY THE ARCHANGEL RAPHAEL TO HELP HIM
BIND THE DEMONS WHO WERE DISRUPTING THE
BUILDING OF THE TEMPLE. THE SIX-POINTED
STAR SYMBOLIZES THE MARRIAGE OF HEAVEN AND
EARTH, THE SYNTHESIS OF ALL ELEMENTS, AND
THUS THE UNION OF OPPOSITES

THE SEAL OF SOLOMON

The Seal of Solomon is a hexagram, a six-pointed star made by two overlapping equilateral triangles. This symbolizes the union of fire and water, the marriage of soul and spirit, sulfur and mercury, the Chemical Wedding. It is the union of the above and the below, the marriage of heaven and earth, the macrocosm and the microcosm, two things becoming one. The harmonious resolution and fusion of opposites represents the completion of the Great Work and corresponds to the six days of Creation, the Great Work of the absolute.

The hexagram is known in Indian alchemy as the *Sri-Yantra*, being the complete interpenetration of Shiva and Shakti, the male and female principles. The alchemist Jacob Boehme called it "the most meaningful sign in the entire universe." He saw it as a symbol of Christ as androgyne, the perfectly balanced, all-reconciling, divine human.

Within the symbol we find the one, which is often emphasized by enclosing it within the ouroboros; the duads of fire and water and above and below; the trinity, implicit in the repeated triangles; and the quaternity of the four elements. Implicit, as well, is the quintessence as the mystical center,

which is found through meditating on the symbol as a mandala. This reveals the hexagram to be another symbol for Mercurius, the agent of dissolution and resolution, without which there would be no beginning or end to the Great Work.

The six points of this "Star of the Wise" denote the six alchemical directions: North, South, East, West, above, and below, which, as pairs, define the three dimensions within which the Great Work takes place.

AS ABOVE, SO BELOW

Astrology and alchemy are very closely connected. Indeed, all alchemists work with aspects of astrology and share its symbols. The Hermetic dictum, "as above, so below," establishes astrology as a central pillar of Hermetic thought. The map of the heavens is a map of the Earth, and those who can read the heavens will understand the workings of all things on the Earth.

The solar system is a single body; the planets, including the Sun and the Moon, are the vital organs of that body and correspond to organs within the human body as well as to archetypes of the human psyche. The balance of planetary attributes that we contain varies from person to person, just as the balance of the four elements (see pages 72–73) varies in all mixtures, including plants and minerals. We may, for example, describe someone as being saturnine or mercurial if they strongly exhibit certain qualities of Saturn or Mercury. Paracelsus emphasizes the planetary correspondences with regard to diseases and medicines. If a patient has a disease of the heart, for example, then it reflects a weakness or imbalance of martial energies, as may also be indicated by a blood problem. The corresponding medicine should therefore be made from a plant ruled by Mars, such as a nettle, or from iron, the metal of Mars. This is what Paracelsus means when he says "Medicine is without value if it is not from Heaven."

Paracelsus repeatedly stresses the importance of working with the stars. As an astrologer, the alchemist, he says, should know the innate nature of the Stars, their complexion and property, as well as a physician understands the nature of a patient, and also the concordance of the Stars, how they stand in relation to men, animals, the four elements, and all things that grow and spring from the matrices of the elements.

In Hermetic philosophy, the seven visible bodies of the solar system (all of which are referred to as "planets," including the Sun and Moon) represent consecutive stages in the unfolding and development of the world. They are often depicted in alchemical art as a ladder that we must climb if we wish to return to the Absolute. The planetary spheres within us must be purified and their challenges met and mastered on the path of return. In the following pages, we will examine the roles and attributes of the seven ruling planetary bodies and how they resonate within us. Lists of correspondences are given, which help us to tune into the energies of the planets and to observe their signs in nature.

As an exercise, it is very helpful to meditate on a planet on its corresponding day. We may contemplate its attributes and correspondences while burning an appropriate incense. Then we can actively visualize the planet's symbol before allowing our minds to empty and passively receive any impressions that may be waiting for us.

THE RAYS OF GOD

The seven rays of the Sun of God shine upon mountains containing the planetary metals. Miners extract the ores and smelt the metals.

SATURN

Saturn is the guardian of the threshold, often portrayed as a dragon, between the material and the spiritual world, where eternity becomes time and space. The most distant and slowest-moving of the visible planets, Saturn is the planet of restriction and inhibition. Saturn can be a severe taskmaster, causing isolation, depression, and calamity until we master ourselves.

In alchemical symbolism, Saturn is presented as the skeletal figure of death or Old Father Time, mercilessly cutting down the old or unworthy with his scythe. This also applies to the impurities of the material with which the alchemist is working, including the corresponding aspects within him- or herself. Encountering this aspect of Saturn represents the initiation of the nadir, the turmoil that ends when we realize that we are doomed unless we commit ourselves to the path of return and abandon folly and frivolity to save our souls. This is where the Great Work begins.

CORRESPONDENCES

PRINCIPLES: *inhibition, concentration.*

DAY OF THE WEEK: *Saturday.*

METAL: *lead.*

ZODIACAL SIGN: *Capricorn.*

ELEMENT: *earth.*

COLORS: *iridescent black, purple. In the Great Work it is the* nigredo, *the black stage.*

PROCESS: *calcination.*

DEITIES: *Cronos/Saturn, Ceridwen.*

CREATURES: *tortoise, beaver, vole, worm, heron, crow, ant, termite.*

STONES: *onyx, jet, diamond, obsidian, black coral, coal.*

INCENSE: *myrrh, spikenard, harmal, copal, aloe, fenugreek.*

PLANTS: *most irises, cornflower, maize.*

TREES: *beech, holly, poplar, Scotch pine, yew.*

HEALING PLANTS: *equisetum, comfrey, verbascum, heartsease, red root, uva ursi.*

BODY PARTS: *bone structure, teeth, tendons, joints, spleen.*

BODY FUNCTIONS: *all hardening and aging processes; blood circulation in tissues.*

MENTAL FUNCTION: *long-term memory.*

MALFUNCTIONS: *rheumatism, depression, lethargy, aging.*

VIRTUES: *discipline, sincerity, humility, perseverance, acceptance, wisdom.*

VICES: *melancholy, crankiness, distrust, isolation, inflexibility, meanness.*

KEYWORD: *saturnine.*

CHILD KILLING DRAGON

Dragons pull stern Saturn's celestial chariot. In the background are Saturnian motifs—
poverty, old age, death, punishment, purification. In the alembic, Mercurius doses the dragon
with poisonous medicine and stokes up the inner fires that will reduce it to ashes.

♃ Jupiter is by far the largest of the visible planets. It has thirteen moons that are attracted by its powerful magnetic field. Its energies are carried to Earth by the solar wind. In contrast to the restrictive and inhibitory qualities of Saturn, Jupiter is expansive, generous, warm, and jovial. Jupiter is the fire of nature, the warmth in all things. In Roman mythology, Jupiter is the lusty, self-indulgent king of the Olympian gods. This tendency to excess is Jupiter's main weakness. As with all of the planets, its qualities can be inverted if badly aspected by others. Jupiter rules harmony, law, and religion.

JUPITER

The alchemical process of sublimation is symbolized by the story in which Jupiter, in the form of an eagle, carries his cup-bearer, Ganymede, up to Heaven. Jupiter's seduction of Danae in the form of a golden shower symbolizes the distillation of philosophical gold.

CORRESPONDENCES

PRINCIPLES: *harmony, justice.*

DAY OF THE WEEK: *Thursday.*

METAL: *tin.*

ZODIACAL SIGN: *Sagittarius and Pisces.*

ELEMENT: *fire.*

COLORS: *mauve, blue, purple. In the Great Work it is the color gray.*

PROCESS: *dissolution.*

DEITIES: *Zeus/Jupiter/Jove, Sobek, Math, Dagda.*

CREATURES: *whale, dolphin, fish, elephant, horse, eagle, water birds, bee.*

STONES: *sapphire, lapis lazuli, amethyst, turquoise, tanzanite, all blue and purple stones.*

INCENSE: *myrrh, sandalwood, benzoin, gum mastic, cedar, fennel, nutmeg.*

PLANTS: *lilac, scarlet pimpernel, carnation, hyacinth, hyssop.*

TREES: *oak, ash, maple, horse chestnut, cedar.*

HEALING PLANTS: *arnica, borage, lemon balm, sage, ginseng, comfrey, mullein, echinacea, dandelion.*

BODY PARTS: *liver, arteries, digestive organs, buttocks, right ear, outer sex organs, feet.*

BODY FUNCTIONS: *immune system, sugar economy, energy conservation, cell formation, food assimilation.*

MENTAL FUNCTIONS: *memory, humor.*

MALFUNCTIONS: *cancer, cirrhosis, stomach ulcers.*

VIRTUES: *generosity, fairness, benevolence, mercy, compassion.*

VICES: *vanity, self-indulgence, greediness, materialism.*

KEYWORD: *jovial (from Jove, Jupiter's alternative name).*

THREE BIRDS

Jupiter presides over benign rulership and justice. The peacocks drawing his chariot refer both to princely splendor and to the stage of the work known as cauda pavonis *("peacock's tail"), heralding the arrival of Mars. Jove's warmth raises the temperature of the alembic to a ferment in which the* Tria Prima *("Three Principles") separate and seethe.*

MARS

The fiery, red "iron planet" represents the intensely masculine, active, dynamic principle. Its effects are intensifying, accelerating, and violent. As the Roman god of war, Mars has a traditional reputation, along with Saturn, as a malign body at conflict with the other planets. The negative aspects of Mars include ruthlessness, destruction, and brutality. Its positive aspects are determination and willpower, courage and passion.

Paracelsus tells us that Mars governs the polarity between the brain pole and the sexual organs. This is the conduit for *Kundalini*, the serpent power in Indian alchemy. Jacob Boehme calls Mars "the wheel of anxiety." In alchemical symbolism Mars is often represented as a warrior wielding a sword. With Venus, Mars is associated with the *cauda pavonis* (peacock's-tail) stage of the Great Work. This dazzling display of colors precedes the *albedo*, the white stage of the Work.

CORRESPONDENCES

PRINCIPLE: *energy.*

DAY OF THE WEEK: *Tuesday.*

METAL: *iron.*

ZODIACAL SIGNS: *Aries and Scorpio.*

ELEMENT: *fire.*

COLOR: *red.*

PROCESS: *separation.*

DEITIES: *Ares/Mars, Tiu/Tyr, Bishamon, all war gods.*

CREATURES: *fox, ram, robin, sparrow, scorpion, all stinging insects other than bees.*

STONES: *ruby, garnet, bloodstone, carnelian, red coral.*

INCENSE: *cypress, aloe, tobacco, pine, red cedar.*

PLANTS: *anemones, geranium, madder, yellow gentian, honeysuckle.*

TREES: *thorn trees, pines, savin, cypress, rhododendron.*

HEALING PLANTS: *hawthorn, nettle, sarsaparilla, vomic nut, basil.*

BODY PARTS: *muscular system, red blood corpuscles, sex organs, gall, astral body.*

BODY FUNCTIONS: *body heat, kundalini, blood formation.*

MENTAL FUNCTION: *left-brain activity.*

MALFUNCTIONS: *fevers, inflammation, high blood pressure, hemorrhage.*

VIRTUES: *courage, determination, passion, protection.*

VICES: *wrath, impulsiveness, ruthlessness, brutality, destructiveness.*

KEYWORD: *martial.*

TRIPLE-HEADED BIRD

The chariot of Mars is drawn by the dogs of war. Its wheels show the zodiacal ram and the
Scorpion. The warmonger puts all to the sword or the torch. The heat generated by the fires of Mars
sublimates the Tria Prima ("Three Principles") which recombine harmoniously in the alembic.

THE SUN

The Sun is vitality and consciousness. It is the individual soul as opposed to the spirit, which is represented by the Moon. In alchemy it is usually referred to by its Latin name, *Sol*. It is equated with gold, the perfected metal, which it evolves to perfection with its heat and transforming rays in the crucible of the Earth. It is often equated with the Red Lion, or Red Tincture, the Philosopher's Stone itself. Paired with the Moon or, as the Red King, with the White Queen, it is sulfur, the hot, dry, masculine principle, the active, engendering seed, called the Father of the Stone.

As a planetary sphere, the Sun's influence is benign, but if overemphasized it can engender pride and self-centeredness. Without the cooling, moistening influence of the Moon, it can be harsh, arid, and burning. In the Great Work it is associated with the processes of coagulation and conjunction. It signifies the *rubedo*, the reddening stage of the Great Work. The Sun rules the heart, circulation, and health.

CORRESPONDENCES

PRINCIPLES: *the soul, consciousness, vitality.*

DAY OF THE WEEK: *Sunday.*

METAL: *gold.*

ZODIACAL SIGN: *Leo.*

ELEMENT: *fire.*

COLORS: *gold, red.*

PROCESSES: *coagulation, conjunction, digestion.*

DEITIES: *Apollo, Helios, Bel, Ra, Mithras.*

CREATURES: *lion, all cats, blackbird, yellow and orange butterflies.*

STONES: *ruby, tiger's eye, amber, chrysolite.*

INCENSE: *frankincense, myrrh, copal, cinnamon, bergamot.*

PLANTS: *peony, marigold, sunflower.*

TREES: *walnut, ash, citrus trees, laurel, juniper.*

HEALING PLANTS: *chamomile, eyebright, Saint John's wort, rosemary.*

BODY PARTS: *heart, spine, solar plexus, eyes.*

BODY FUNCTIONS: *circulation, heat and energy distribution.*

MENTAL FUNCTION: *mental organization.*

MALFUNCTIONS: *low vitality, cardiac problems.*

VIRTUES: *health, vitality, organization, power.*

VICES: *pride, egotism.*

KEYWORD: *solar.*

TRIPLE-HEADED DRAGON

The single wheel of the Sun's chariot indicates its rulership of Leo the lion. In the alembic the matter has now incorporated pronounced leonine aspects. The heads show the colors that mark the principle stages of the Work: albedo (white), rubedo (red), and nigredo (black).

VENUS

Venus is the planet of love, the muse of art, friendship, and music. As the ruler of the zodiacal sign of Libra, Venus helps to mediate between opposites and to integrate diverse elements into a harmonious balance. We think of Venus as the Roman goddess of love, known as Aphrodite to the Ancient Greeks, but to the Egyptians, Indians, and Hebrews this planetary deity is masculine. To the Indians it is the male god Sukra, who has some of the attributes of the Egyptian Thoth, being a teacher and physician. Legend relates that Sukra possessed the Elixir of Immortality, known in Western alchemy as the White Lion or White Stone. This associates Venus closely with alchemy.

Venus rules important organs and functions within the human body, including the kidneys, the inner sexual organs, blood and cell formation, and the sense of smell. Venus is associated with the process of fermentation and the *cauda pavonis* ("peacock's-tail") display of colors during the Great Work.

CORRESPONDENCES

PRINCIPLES: *love, art.*

DAY OF THE WEEK: *Friday.*

METAL: *copper.*

ZODIACAL SIGNS: *Libra, Taurus.*

ELEMENT: *air.*

COLORS: *rose, emerald.*

PROCESS: *fermentation.*

DEITIES: *Venus/Aphrodite, Sukra, Ishtar, Benten, Lakshmi, Chenrezi.*

CREATURES: *deer, rabbit, dove, swallow, butterfly.*

STONES: *emerald, rose quartz, opal, jade, malachite, pink coral.*

INCENSE: *sandalwood, storax, galbanum, valerian, violet.*

PLANTS: *red/pink roses, orchid, primrose, violet, columbine.*

TREES: *apple, pear, cherry, elder, linden, chestnut.*

HEALING PLANTS: *yarrow, lady's mantle, motherwort, vervain.*

BODY PARTS: *complexion, upper lip, throat, breasts, kidneys, abdomen, inner sexual organs.*

BODY FUNCTIONS: *cell and nerve formation, diuretic and emetic processes, sense of smell.*

MENTAL FUNCTIONS: *artistic creativity.*

MALFUNCTIONS: *problems relating to the sexual organs and kidneys.*

VIRTUES: *harmony, proportion, beauty, affection.*

VICES: *sentimentality, immodesty, tastelessness, sexual intemperance.*

KEYWORD: *Venusian.*

THE PEACOCK

*Venus arrives, drawn by a pair of love birds with a figure of Cupid/Eros on
the prow. People are engaging in the sensual activities over which she presides—
music, dance, courtship, and merriment. In the alembic we are treated to
the gorgeous display of the peacock, a sign that the Work is proceeding well.*

The planet Mercury is the fastest-moving planet; the quicksilver messenger service mediating between the above and the below. It rules mental processes, language, communications, adaptability, and the intellect. It has an ambivalent quality, akin to the trickster figures in some traditions, who sets pitfalls for people to show them their foolishness. Anyone who has done any practical laboratory alchemy will know only too well the tricks that Mercurius can play to distract, trip, or upset. It forces us to bring all of our faculties to bear in a state of full alertness.

MERCURY

As the planet and god, Mercury should not be confused with the mercury of the sulfur–mercury duad. As a planetary entity, Mercury is androgynous, containing all opposites within itself. It is therefore a free operator, independent of a polar opposite, although it does have an antagonistic relationship with Saturn. This is symbolized by a child (Mercury) killing a dragon (Saturn), initiating the Great Work by dispatching the forces that imprison the *prima materia*.

CORRESPONDENCES

PRINCIPLES: *mediation, intelligence.*

DAY OF THE WEEK: *Wednesday.*

METAL: *quicksilver (mercury).*

ZODIACAL SIGNS: *Gemini, Virgo.*

ELEMENT: *air.*

COLORS: *orange, yellow.*

PROCESS: *distillation, circulation.*

DEITIES: *Mercury/Hermes, Thoth, Quetzalcoatl, Viracocha, Kukulkan.*

CREATURES: *coyote, monkeys, raven, ibis, fly.*

STONES: *opal, topaz, tourmaline, carnelian, peridot.*

INCENSE: *anise, lavender, gum arabic, storax.*

PLANTS: *azalea, red foxglove, lily of the valley, elecampane.*

TREES: *hazel, acacia, myrtle, mulberry*

HEALING PLANTS: *wormwood, mandrake, valerian, skullcap, parsley.*

BODY PARTS: *ears, tongue, nervous system, hands, feet, lungs, spinal chord, thyroid.*

BODY FUNCTIONS: *mental and nervous processes, hearing, speech, respiration, coordination.*

MENTAL FUNCTION: *intellect, faculty of speech.*

MALFUNCTIONS: *impairment of nerves and motor functions, speech impediments, dyslexia.*

VIRTUES: *communication, mediation, sound judgment, diplomacy.*

VICES: *trickery, coldness, miserliness, mental cruelty.*

KEYWORD: *mercurial.*

THE VIRGIN

The appearance of the White Queen is heralded by Mercury and his crowing cockerels.
Although a pure virgin, she has conceived and bears the royal child of the Sun. She is
the albedo, the Elixir, one stage away from absolute perfection, but quite incorruptible.

THE MOON

The Moon rules the emotions, instincts, and the subconscious. It is feminine, nurturing, reflective, and changeable. It influences fertility, growth, and conception. The waters of the oceans, the sap in plants, and all bodily fluids are influenced by the Moon, as witnessed by the tides and women's menstrual cycles. Everything that grows upon the earth does so in rhythm with the Moon.

The Moon rules dreams, the emotions, sensuality, intuition, and the way we feel. Its dark side is the unconscious, the wilder, baser instincts. It is the bride of the Sun, often called by its Latin name, *Luna*, or Diana, the lunar goddess of the Romans. It is also mercury to the Sun's sulfur, the cold, moist, passive, feminine principle that receives the seed of sulfur and bears the hermaphroditic child. Physiologically, it rules the stomach, cerebellum, and pancreas. The Moon is most closely associated with the alchemical processes of coagulation and conjunction and is a symbol for the White Lion or the White Stone, the Elixir of Immortality.

CORRESPONDENCES

PRINCIPLES: *the feminine principle, spirit.*

DAY OF THE WEEK: *Monday.*

METAL: *silver.*

ZODIACAL SIGN: *Cancer.*

ELEMENT: *water.*

COLORS: *silver, violet, royal purple.*

PROCESSES: *conjunction, coagulation.*

DEITIES: *Isis, Artemis, Diana, Selene, Cybele, Arianrhod, Astarte.*

CREATURES: *shellfish, wolf, owl, nightingale, nightjar, moth, spider.*

STONES: *moonstone, pearl, aquamarine.*

INCENSE: *camphor, jasmine, ylang-ylang.*

PLANTS: *white lilies, acanthus, water lily, pale irises.*

TREES: *willow, magnolia.*

HEALING PLANTS: *chaste tree, cleavers, opium poppy, periwinkle.*

BODY PARTS: *brain, womb, bladder, stomach, pancreas, body fluids.*

BODY FUNCTIONS: *menstruation, growth, fertility, glandular secretion.*

MENTAL FUNCTIONS: *memory, subconscious, instinct, intuition, reflection, dreaming.*

MALFUNCTIONS: *psychosis, schizophrenia, lycanthropy.*

VIRTUES: *sensitivity, motherliness, benevolence.*

VICES: *moodiness, impressionability, hypersensitivity, defensiveness.*

KEYWORDS: *lunar, feeling.*

THE RED KING

Luna, the ruler of Cancer, the mother, arrives in a chariot drawn by two midwives. She has given birth to the Red King, the sum of all perfection, the Stone itself, whose golden orb and scepter, robe of royal purple and golden aura proclaim his absolute majesty.

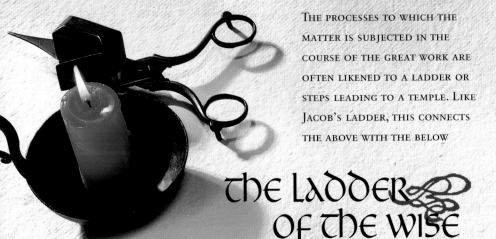

THE PROCESSES TO WHICH THE
MATTER IS SUBJECTED IN THE
COURSE OF THE GREAT WORK ARE
OFTEN LIKENED TO A LADDER OR
STEPS LEADING TO A TEMPLE. LIKE
JACOB'S LADDER, THIS CONNECTS
THE ABOVE WITH THE BELOW

THE LADDER OF THE WISE

The Great Work consists of various stages and processes. In alchemical literature, these stages are almost invariably presented as laboratory processes, which are described using highly complex imagery, both verbal and graphic. In such treatises as J. D. Mylius's *Philosophia Reformata* and Solomon Trismosin's *Splendor Solis*, the text and graphics bear little apparent relationship to one another. For the alchemist working on the inner plane, the imagery of alchemical emblems can often speak more eloquently than their accompanying text. Such emblems usually offer up their meaning over time when meditated on repeatedly, particularly when series of images are considered as a whole, as well as in isolation. In alchemy, context is everything.

Some authors give the number of stages in the Great Work as twelve, fourteen, or even twenty-two, but the most common number is probably seven. These seven stages do not necessarily correspond exactly to the seven planets, although such correspondences can often be made. Being a mysterious and inexact science, alchemy tends to be suggestive rather than discursive. It is also important to bear in mind that the order of the various processes is almost always deliberately muddled by alchemical authors. There are two obvious reasons for this: one is to confuse the merely curious and profane; the other is that such processes do not necessarily lead from one to another in a predetermined way, particularly on the inner level. To give an obvious example: a certain understanding that may seem obvious to you may elude others whom you consider wiser than yourself. Some of the processes may not even be necessary in order to achieve perfection, although seven distinct stages is probably the minimum number required.

The processes and accompanying emblems that are described in the following pages may be interpreted in many different ways. We experience them in the context of our own highly personal and subjective lives. My comments should therefore be considered only suggestions that may stimulate the reader's own intuition. You may make any correspondences you like because none are necessarily invalid.

What I do suggest, however, is that the emblems be allowed to speak for themselves. Let the images interpret you. By allowing them to seep into your being, they can animate your subconscious and come alive in your dreams and meditations to transmit very personal messages. They may even initiate the very processes that they describe. Because this can be a very powerful, and somewhat alarming, experience, be sure to trust the process and to allow the spirit to move within you.

THE STAGES OF PERFECTION

The Philosopher ferrets out the prima materia *buried deep within the mountain. The Ladder of the Wise leads to the inner temple containing the purified principles. Atop the temple is the phoenix, symbol of the Stone.*

TO CALCINE A SUBSTANCE MEANS TO BURN IT UNTIL ALL HAS TURNED CHALKY WHITE. WHEN THIS STAGE IS REACHED THE SUBSTANCE CAN BE ALTERED NO FURTHER BY VULGAR FIRE ALONE. IN ALCHEMY, CALCINATION IS ALWAYS CONSIDERED A PURIFICATION PROCESS

The alchemist in his laboratory points at a blazing athenor in which a calcination is taking place. This process involves burning a substance to ashes and symbolizes the secret fire that destroys all aspects of false personality. There is no escape for the ego. If it resists, the fire will only be stoked up hotter.

All our purifications are done in fire, by fire, and with fire.
THE MYSTERY OF THE CATHEDRALS

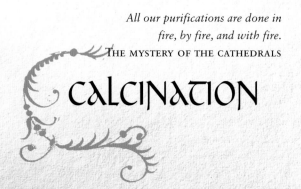

CALCINATION

A lion is devouring a snake. The lion is the sulfur, the raw, inner fire of the soul; the serpent is unrefined mercury, the unclean, false spirit that starves the soul and poisons the ego with selfishness. The lion symbolizes the soul's hunger and the courage and strength necessary to seize and destroy the deceiver. The wily serpent will twist and turn to save itself, blaming everything but itself, resorting at last to self-pity. The purifying fire is merciless, but only falseness dies.

The ashes contain the salt of the stone, the key to the next stage. We see this in the two flowers growing out of the crucible on the table. Seated at the table are the Sun and the Moon. They, too, are sulfur and mercury, but refined, exalted, and harmonious. They are the heavenly, immortal soul and spirit. They wear armor, protecting the alchemist's true self, who is none other than winged Hermes, delighting in the progress of the Great Work.

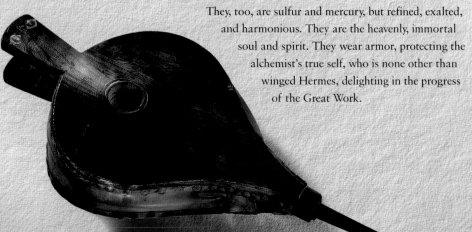

THE SECRETS OF FIRES

"Natural fire...is that which is fed with fuel, and feeds a flame. So
become acquainted with the secrets of fires, and the true achievements
of our Medicine, which lead easily to the achievement of the
Magistery." Mylius, Philosophia reformata, 1622.

DISSOLUTION

DISSOLUTION IS THE SECOND
MAJOR OPERATION IN THE
ALCHEMY OF TRANSFORMATION.
IT IS THE *SOLVE* OF THE
ALCHEMICAL LAW *SOLVE ET
COAGULA*— "DISSOLVE (THE
BODY) AND COAGULATE/BIND/FIX
(THE SPIRIT)." FOR THE BODY
TO BE PERMEATED BY SPIRIT IT
MUST FIRST BE DISSOLVED

I was thirsty and ye gave me drink.
ST. MATTHEW 25:35

When we calcinate a plant, we are left with nothing
but pale ashes. Within these ashes, however, is the *sal
salis*, the salt of the earth, the matrix of the true self.
This salt is strongly hygroscopic, sucking out of the

MAN OF FIRE

"Then the fiery man will sweat And become hot in the fire; Also he will resolve his body And carry it afar through moisture." Daniel Stolcius, Chemisches Lustgaertlein, 1625.

air the moisture that it needs in order to dissolve, thereby becoming a powerfully corrosive solution. The water contains the fire that allows the salt to burn. Dame Nature points to water springing from a rock beneath the lion's feet. The snake's poison has burned through the lion and has reduced it to ashes, but the water has raised the lion from the dead. The Green Lion leaps greedily at the Sun. Now it has the power to dissolve gold.

Our Lady admonishes it, pointing to the ground, where water springs from under a stone. This is what the Green Lion needs in order to give it teeth. The resurrected man points to the womblike vessel, which is receiving water distilled by the furnace. He has drunk from the stream and radiates strength and joy.

The Green Lion is our Mercury, still in an unperfected state. It is the initiate, who has been tried by fire and is eager for more solar consciousness, the bright light of illumination. But the soul can only grow if it allows itself to receive the grace that is now its due. We must respond to the feminine: cool down, absorb, and reflect in order to dissolve. Reduced to ashes, we dissolve into tears. Our tears sprinkle on our roasting ashes, making them whiter, redeeming us, dissolving the pain. When there is no more pain, the process is over. We have miraculously survived; we are naked, but connected with our soul. The love of the universe, personified by Dame Nature, has come to our rescue. We are known. We are cared for. Our thirst is slaked and our spirits are revived. We are empowered, able to dissolve any obstacles.

LEGEND HAS IT THAT HERMES USED TO CARRY A PLAIN WAND UNTIL ONE DAY HE
CAME ACROSS TWO FIGHTING SNAKES. HE SEPARATED THEM WITH HIS WAND, WHEREUPON
THEY COILED THEMSELVES HARMONIOUSLY AROUND IT, FORMING THE CADUCEUS.
WE MUST IDENTIFY WITH THE HERMES WITHIN OURSELVES AND BECOME RECONCILED

The fire of calcination gives
way to the water of dissolution.
Now the element of air takes
over. A man and a woman are
in conflict. The man defends
himself with sword and shield,
while the woman has an eagle on her arm, ready to
fly at the man. Hermes separates the polarized couple,
armed with a caduceus in each hand, reminding them
that they are both responsible for reconciling the
polarities within themselves. What has gone wrong?

Separate the pure from the impure;
the subtle from the gross.
ALCHEMICAL DICTUM

After the purifying and revivifying processes of calcination and dissolution, all had seemed to
be well. Unfortunately, the Philosopher's Stone is not so easily made. If crashing and burning,
followed by a good cry, were enough to achieve enlightenment, we'd all be adepts by puberty.

Separation occurs when our spirits and souls (or wills) are not in
harmony. Following the surrender of dissolution, the spirit feels
antagonized and attacks the will. The solution that we have
become is corrosive and as sharp as the man's sword and the
eagle's beak. It is vitriolic and attacks everything that it
contains. But the dross that was burned off is insoluble.
It must be separated, filtered off.

Diana points to the ground. If we aspiring adepts are to
put on our wings, then that which is an obstacle to our
development must be removed, cast to the ground, or
else it will irritate us, becoming a bone of contention
over which our souls and spirits will fight. Separation
can be an extremely painful process, but the
emblem shows us how to deal with it.

We must identify with the Hermes within ourselves and become reconciled like the caduceus. The sword and the eagle are both symbols of the element of air, which corresponds to the intellect, cognitive imagination, and breathing. Hermes here warns us against allowing our minds to torture ourselves. By the use of breath and imagination, we can resolve our inner conflict. The caduceus meditation (see page 22) is the true solution.

(see page 22)

THE WARRING ELEMENTS WITHIN

"On this third rung of the ladder of the Wise, the four warring elements previously mentioned and distinguished from each other, are separated by a rectifying distillation, therefore the third step is called Our Separation." Mylius, Philosophia reformata, 1622.

THE WARRING COUPLE WHO WERE SEPARATED BY A YOUTHFUL,
ARMORED HERMES ARE NOW CONJOINED IN HOLY MATRIMONY BY
THE MATURE HERMES WE RECOGNIZE FROM THE FIRST STAGE OF
THE WORK. AFTER CONJUNCTION, THE ADEPT IS ABLE TO DISCERN
WHAT NEEDS TO BE DONE TO ACHIEVE LASTING ENLIGHTENMENT,
WHICH IS UNION WITH THE DIVINE

Make one water out of two waters.
ROSARIUM PHILOSOPHORUM

CONJUNCTION

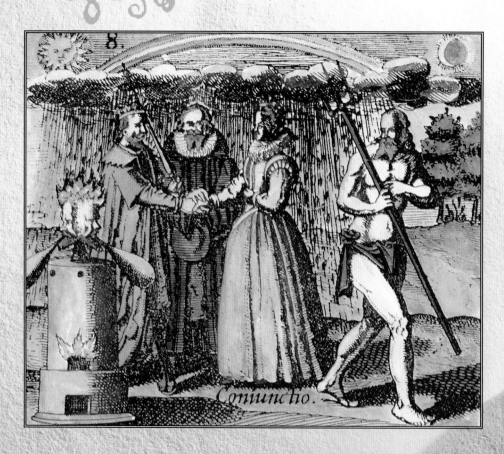

Coniunctio.

Now reconciled, sulfur and mercury are conjoined in harmony, represented here by a wedding. Neptune's three-pronged trident punctures the clouds and a shower of rain purifies the royal couple. *Sol* and *Luna*, fire and water, combine to produce a rainbow, which arches over the lovers, symbolizing the meeting of heaven and earth and reconciliation. The rainbow's seven colors represent the seven planets in harmony, as well as the Trinity and the elements. In mineral alchemical work, the rain signifies the washing of the matter before the appearance of the peacock's tail, the *cauda pavonis*, with its display of colors. To the Italian poet Dante, the rainbow symbolized Christ, "by whom we are protected from spiritual flood." The double-headed furnace is the inner fire that distills the essence that nourishes both spirit and soul.

The initiate has achieved a state of inner equilibrium, is conscious of the opposing principles within him- or herself, and is able to balance and reconcile them. This development in consciousness is symbolized by the crowns on the couple's heads. The initiate has attained a degree of power, but the immortality of true enlightenment has not yet been won.

UNITE AGAIN COMPLETELY

Hermes unites the couple, but his dual nature is revealed by his forked beard and echoed in the Janus-faced head above the furnace. He smiles on the lovers, but knows that their union will precipitate their death.

IN SPAGYRICS THE PROCESS OF FERMENTATION IS CALLED "PUTREFACTION." THE
BODY OF THE PLANT DIES, ITS DREGS FALLING TO THE BOTTOM OF THE VESSEL.
IN SO DOING, HOWEVER, ALCOHOL IS PRODUCED—THE BODY GIVES UP ITS SPIRIT.
THIS CARRIES WITH IT THE PLANT'S ESSENCE, ITS SOUL, WHICH IS RESURRECTED
THROUGH DISTILLATION, THE NEXT PROCESS IN THE ALCHEMICAL OPERATION

FERMENTATION

The process of fermentation, or putrefaction, is the initiate's "long, dark night of the soul," the descent into darkness, the metaphysical death. This "black that is blacker than black" (*nigrum nigrius nigra*) is symbolized by the raven.

This is the preparation which they call the change and the division…
ROSARIUM PHILOSOPHORUM

Sol and *Luna*, conjoined in marriage in the previous emblem, are now eclipsed by their own conjunction. Their leavening passion, imbibed with the rain, has set the pair in ferment. This produces a spirit, a philosophical mercury, that dissolves the body that contained them. In becoming something greater through their union, they lose their identities, but do not entirely cease to be: they are dead, but not in the grave. The skeleton stands above the eclipsed pair. Though fleshless and anonymous, Death has already been resurrected. The angels watch over the process, honoring the sacredness of even this most hellish scene. A tree has been felled, yet there is life in it and a new branch sprouts from the stump. On this side of the river all is stygian black, but on the other bank the sun shines, the steeple soars, and all is alive.

This *nigredo*, the black phase, is the shaman's death, a dangerous and terrifying ordeal that the initiate can only survive if he or she is sufficiently balanced. Without the inner equilibrium attained in the conjunction, the initiate is prey to schizophrenia, amnesia, paralysis, catalepsy, and even real death. This is a time for guardian angels. If the initiate has earned his or her spurs, the reward will be a mystical *palingenesis*, a rebirth in which the soul is truly born with the chance of immortality.

THE SPIRIT RENEWED

"*Destruction brings about Death of the material;*
But the spirit renews, Like before, the life.
Provided that the seed is Putrefied in the right soil;
Otherwise all labor, work, and art Will be in vain."
Daniel Stolcius, Chemisches Lustgaertlein, 1625.

The alchemist in red and his soror mystica ("mystic sister") in white are using an elegant distillation train, shaped like the caduceus of Hermes, to distill aqua vitae ("water of life").

Distillation is one of the key processes in alchemy. There are several different types of distillation. In the Lesser Work, the sulfur and mercury are distilled into a purified form and are kept carefully, while the remaining mass is calcined and filtered to collect the *sal sulfuris*, the precious salts, which are later recombined with the sulfur and mercury. In the Great Work, the form of distillation employed is a circulation, a process that occurs within the hermetically sealed alembic. Through gentle heating, the volatile elements are transmuted into air; they condense at the top of the vessel, becoming water, and descend again like tears, to rise again through the action of fire to repeat the process.

It rises from Earth to Heaven and descends again to Earth, thereby combining within Itself the powers of both the Above and the Below.
THE EMERALD TABLET

DISTILLATION

THE ART OF DISTILLATION WAS INVENTED BY ALCHEMISTS. IT RELEASES VOLATILE ESSENCES FROM THEIR MATERIAL BONDS, RECONDENSING THEM IN A PURIFIED FORM. THROUGH DISTILLATION WE CAN PURIFY SPIRIT AND SOUL

SUBLIMATION

In this way, the fixed becomes volatile and the volatile becomes fixed. With each circulation, the matter is farther exalted, "combining the power of above and below." Sometimes called a rotation, distillation can be compared to the movement of a wheel: if it is grounded and set on its axis correctly, each turn of the wheel moves it farther down the road. The Great Work is a pilgrimage, moving slowly, but conscientiously, toward its goal. Immense patience and faith may be required. There is no more separating or filtering to be done. Everything is precious and indispensable, no matter how onerous it may seem, so nothing can be rejected and all must be embraced and integrated. This requires great love. Alchemists also call this process sublimation.

The raven of putrefaction has become a white dove, a symbol of faith and peace, the purified soul, and spiritual forces.

COAGULATION

Solve et coagula.
(*"Dissolve and coagulate."*)
ALCHEMICAL DICTUM

COAGULATION IS THE PRECIPITATION
OF THE PURIFIED FERMENT FROM
DISTILLATION. IT IS ACHIEVED WHEN
THE SECRET FIRE OF THE PRIMA MATERIA
HAS BEEN LIBERATED FROM ITS MATERIAL
BONDS AND PURIFIED, WHILE CONTAINED
WITHIN THE ALEMBIC

The final stage of the Great Work is accomplished when no more changes can be observed occurring within the matter. We have subjected it to many ordeals; we have purified it and have provided it with the ideal conditions within which to exalt itself. Now the Philosopher's Stone has been perfected. It is no longer subject to change, but is immutable and incorruptible. It has a waxy, yet powdery, consistency and a crystalline quality. It is bright, and yet not translucent. Its color combines all of the colors of the Sun. It has the weight of gold. It has a subtle, but penetrating, mysteriously attractive odor, as though it were transmuting the air that touches it into the scent of heaven. The salt of the Earth and the salt of heaven have become the same thing; the serpent and the lion are one. It will only change when projected on to molten metal, whereupon everything changes into gold, a rich, soft, malleable gold of the utmost purity.

The miracle has occurred: a human being has cared enough to prove that all is true and that all is one. The initiate has become the adept, transcending his or her own mortality and gender. The initiate's will is now at one with the Trinity, and his or her hands hold the power of the Universe. The world has been redeemed.

POTABLE GOLD

The glory of the Macrocosm is reflected in the earthly paradise of the Microcosm. The Tree of Life provides all the fruits necessary to produce the Elixir. This superb engraving celebrates the perfecting of the legendary Aurum potabile *("potable gold"), personified by a united Sol and Luna, who appear in their naked glory before Hermes the alchemist.*

CHAPTER IV
SPAGYRICS

S pagyrics is a process of making alchemical tinctures and potions, in which herbs or minerals are separated, purified, and then recombined. Spagyric processing was created by the great sixteenth century healer Paracelsus (see pages 34–37). He coined the word Spagyric from two Greek words, meaning "separate" and "recombine." It is traditional for aspiring alchemists to begin their initiation into laboratory practice with the Vegetable Work. Working with plants is an ideal way to enter the realm of practical hermetic philosophy. To begin with, we need no specialized equipment. Some elementary botany and the spirit of Paracelsus will get us out into the natural world, engaging with nature's creatures, for plants are, indeed, creatures. They have souls, spirits, and emotional responses, as well as a whole host of mysterious intelligent mechanisms. Many exemplify the doctrine of signatures (see page 36), indicating quite clearly through their appearance their therapeutic virtues. Plants speak to us in subtle ways. We are drawn to different flowers and scents, thereby indicating our own signatures and predispositions.

As we have seen, all things, all mixtures, are made up of varying proportions of the four elements and are governed in their responses to greater or lesser degrees by all of the

cabala and alchemy give thee medicine most high

planets. In plants, we find that the influence of one planet usually dominates. Making elixirs from such plants allows us to ingest the energies of the individual planets, purifying and balancing their corresponding spheres within ourselves.

SATURN THE GARDENER

Saturn waters the orchard containing solar and lunar trees.
This refers to an alchemical process called imbibing, which is crucial in
the Circulatum minus *of Baron Urbigerus. In the foreground is the 17th-century*
Moravian alchemist Michael Sendivogius, who performed many transmutations.

PLANTS AND THE THREE PRINCIPLES

In plants, we find the three philosophical principles clearly defined.

We can tell lavender and roses apart with our eyes closed, for they are differentiated by the perfume that characterizes their essential oils. These oils are the essence of a plant, its sulfur principle, its soul.

We call ethyl alcohol spirit because that is what it is: the mercury principle, the spirit of plants. All plants are naturally fermentable. Given the right conditions, the wild yeasts that bloom on leaves and fruit will start to break down the plant sugars, fermenting them and producing alcohol. Pure alcohol is undifferentiated: unlike essential oils it is the same from all plants. It has no individual signature because spirit is anonymous. It is the breath of life that is the same in all things, although its vehicles differ. In the plant kingdom, its vehicle is ethyl alcohol.

The salt, or body, principle in plants is to be found in the water-soluble alkaline salts that reside within the tissues of plants. These must be extracted and purified in order to "resurrect" a plant.

By extracting, purifying, and recombining the soul, spirit, and body of a plant, we "exalt" it, raising its powers to a higher level. The resulting elixir, when ingested, is able to resonate with our spirits, souls, and bodies. Remedies not prepared in this fashion are invariably bereft of at least one of the three principles.

THE SPIN OF THE HEAVENS

Nature spins the sphere of the heavens, at the center of which is the Earth, acted upon by celestial influences.

PARACELSUS TAUGHT THAT ANCIENT AND SECRET BODIES OF KNOWLEDGE WERE TO BE
FOUND "IN JUNIPER, IN MELISSA, IN TINCTURE, IN VITRIOL, AND IN SALT," AND IT IS FROM
THIS BELIEF THAT THE FAITH IN PLANTS AS "MEDICINES FOR THE SOUL" STEMS

SEVEN PLANETARY ELIXIRS

Let us make seven spagyric tinctures, one for
each of the planets and each day of the week.
You will need the following items:
- a field guide to wild flowers and plants
  to help you to identify them correctly
- a book on herbal medicine to make
  sure that you use nothing poisonous
  or contraindicated
- a large pestle and mortar
- ¼ pint (250 ml) spirit of wine—
  for example, brandy or cognac
- at least two large, glass jars, the larger
  about 4–5 inches (10–12 cm) wide
  and at least twice as tall
- a funnel, preferably made of glass
- coffee-filter papers or absorbent cotton
- a high-temperature-resistant, ceramic
  cooking pot, with a capacity of at least
  2 pints (1 liter)
- a dust mask (optional)
- a steel spoon

- a gas-fuelled
  camping stove
- 3 pints (1.5 liters)
  of distilled water
- a glass flask or bottle,
  preferably made of dark glass

THE START OF THE WORK

*The Work begins with the death of the separate
planets (center top); in harmony with the stars,
represented by the zodiac signs, the planets are
united in their dance around the resurrected Sun.
On the Sun's face, the symbols for Leo (the lion)
and omega (the end) mirror each other.*

JOHAN-DANIELIS MYLII
Philofophiæ et Medicinæ
Doctoris,
ANATOMIA AURI,
five
TYROCINIUM MEDICO-
CHYMICUM.
FRANCOFURTI,
Sumptibus LUCÆ JENNISI.

Gloria ac Divitiæ infinitæ

Longitudo dierum et fanitas

the ELIXIR OF SATURN

We shall begin on a Saturday, the day of Saturn, for
this is the sphere within us that we should purify first
of all. Without a balanced relationship with Saturn, we
are prone to depression, accidents, and eccentricity.

First we need to choose a herb that is governed by Saturn (see
Saturn's correspondences on page 80). If we can find one that is
growing wild in an unpolluted area, so much the better. An ideal,
and typical, Saturn herb that is usually widely distributed and easy
to identify is *Equisetum arvense*, commonly known as horsetail,
scouring rush, or shave-brush. As its signature suggests, being

Sheltered by tall trees the corn grows straight and tall.
Saturn is closely associated with plants and agriculture,
being the ruler of the cycle of the seasons. The celestial
reaper harvests the ripened corn with his scythe.

jointed and skeletal in appearance, it is wonderful for keeping
bones strong. Whichever plant we use, we should be sure to
identify it carefully and to familiarize ourselves with its
properties in a good herb book.

harvesting

1. Harvest about 4 lb (2 kg) of the herb on a fine Saturday morning,
after the dew has dried and when the plant is in its prime. The period
around full Moon is usually the best. This is when the plant's vitality is in the stems
and leaves, with the sap running high. Never pick too much from one spot and always
harvest gratefully, and with consideration for the well-being of the species. The more
contact that you can establish with the plant, the better.

desiccation and pulverization

2. The harvested plant matter should now be carefully dried, or *desiccated*. Many plants are
actually improved by drying because all that the plant loses is water, which allows for a more
concentrated tincture. The following Saturday, *pulverize* the herb to a powder in a pestle and
mortar. Before beginning the work, which can be quite tiring, meditate on what you are
doing and why. Energize yourself so that you feel positive and focused. Start to grind the
herb methodically and carefully, being efficient with your energy. (You may need to wear a
dust mask to avoid breathing in too much dust.) You may not be able to grind the larger stalks
down, in which case you can set them aside. Put 8 oz (250 g) of the ground herb into a glass
jar and seal it tightly. The rest, including any discarded stalks, can be placed in a paper bag
and kept in a dry place.

maceration

3. Maceration, the next phase of the work, should be performed on the first Saturday of the
waxing Moon. Try to awake at dawn and to begin the work soon after sunrise, having previously

CORAL

"As the coral grows below the waters and hardens in the air, so does the Stone." The coral must be dried before its tincture is extracted. Emblem 32 of Atalanta fugiens, Michael Maier, 1618.

meditated and stoked up plenty of calm, positive energy. Place the 8 oz (250 g) of the ground herb that you stored in a jar in a larger jar, about 4–5 inches (10–12 cm) wide and at least twice as tall. Slowly pour on the spirit of wine, pausing every now and then to allow the plant powder to absorb it. Stop adding alcohol as soon as it has covered the plant powder by a clear ¼ inches (6 mm). Hermetically seal the jar, that is, make it air-tight, to enable the seal of Hermes to allow nothing in or out. The spirit of wine will draw both the sulfur and mercury principles out of the plant, releasing its soul and spirit.

maceration and circulation

4. Place the jar in a paperboard box, put it in a warm place, and allow the mixture to macerate for two weeks. Droplets of alcohol will condense on the side of the jar and will trickle back down again, as in a circulation.

filtration

5. Two weeks later, on a Saturday, *filter* the tincture into a clean, dry flask or bottle (preferably made of dark glass), using a glass funnel lined with filter paper (a coffee-filter paper will do) or a pad of absorbent cotton. When all of the tincture has dripped through, seal the flask or bottle and place it in a cool, dark, safe place. Put the plant residue into a heat-resistant ceramic pot or dish.

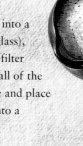

calcination

6. The next phase of the work is the process called calcination. This should be performed outside because it involves burning the remaining plant matter, which produces a lot of acrid smoke. Place the camping stove on the ground in a sheltered spot. Light it and then turn it up to full blast. Place the ceramic pot containing all of the plant matter (including the greater part that was not macerated) on top. The plant matter will start to smoke and turn black. Stir it with a steel spoon. When everything has stopped smoking and has turned black, turn off the stove.

7. Grind the black plant cinders to a powder using a pestle and mortar. Return them to the ceramic pot. The calcination can continue inside. Calcine ("make white") until everything has turned into a gray-white ash.

THE ALLEGORY OF THE KING

The King swimming in the sea, crying aloud: "Whoever saves me will obtain a great reward." The soul/sulfur/essential oil must be carefully extracted and preserved.

solution and separation

8. Add 2 pints (1 liter) of the distilled water to the cool, calcined plant ashes, place a lid over the top, and bring the *solution* to a gentle boil. After about twenty minutes, turn off the heat and allow the liquid to cool. Now filter the ash-and-water solution into a bowl or bottle. The insoluble ashes are known as the *caput mortuum*, or death head. You have *separated* the essential matter from the dross and can now discard the ashes outside if you wish.

purification

9. Clean out the ceramic pot and then return the filtrate (the filtered solution) to it. Heat the filtrate gently, keeping it just below boiling point. The solution will gradually evaporate to leave behind water-soluble, alkaline salts. These are the *sal salis*, the salt of the salt. When the salts are completely dry, turn up the heat, place a lid over the top, and calcine the salts for at least an hour. The sal salis forms white crystals when it is pure, but they will probably need further purification. Add a cup of distilled water to the cooled salts, gently heat the mixture, and stir until everything has dissolved. Cool and filter, and then evaporate and calcine, as before. Repeat this process until the salt crystals are of a uniformly white (or very pale pink) color.

cohobation

10. When the salts have been purified, place them in the large macerating jar (on a Saturday) and carefully pour over the tincture. Through cohobation the three principles are thus reunited in a purified form. Hermetically seal the jar and put it in a warm, dark place.

After two weeks, carefully pour the spagyric tincture into a dark-glass bottle of an appropriate size (the bottle should be full or nearly full), and seal it tightly (perhaps with a sterilized wine cork). You may notice that the aroma of the tincture has changed slightly, along with its color. Your spagyric tincture is now ready. Take seven drops in water or wine three times a day, starting on the first Saturday of a New Moon.

TOOLS OF ALCHEMY

The regulation of heat is crucial in the laboratory. Here we see a number of different athanors (ovens) providing varying degrees of heat, including a sand bath and water baths (called bain-marie after Mary the Jewess).

THE WORD "ELIXIR" IS ONE OF THE MOST AMBIGUOUS WORDS IN ALCHEMY. ITS MEANING CAN RANGE FROM "VITAL SPIRIT," "ESSENTIAL PRINCIPLE," OR "QUINTESSENCE" TO MERCURY, "POTION FOR LONG LIFE," AND THE PHILOSOPHER'S STONE

THE OTHER PLANETARY ELIXIRS

Now you can start preparing the six other planetary elixirs—Jupiter, Mars, The Sun, Venus, Mercury, and The Moon. These can be prepared over the same period as the elixir of Saturn.

Refer to the correspondences of each planet (see pages 82–92) to choose the healing herbs that you wish to work with. If you are not sure which ones to use, some recommendations follow.

HAWTHORN

CLEAVERS

CARAWAY

LEMON BALM

SKULLCAP

MOTHERWORT

HORSETAIL

ROSEMARY

the elixir of jupiter

Lemon balm is traditionally used for the Jupiter elixir. If you cannot find it growing wild, you could grow it yourself, beg some from a friend's garden, or buy it dried from a good herb supplier.

the elixir of mars

Hawthorn (the flowers, young leaves, or berries) and dried nettle root (pulled up during a waning Moon) are both good choices for the elixir of Mars.

the elixir of the sun

Rosemary is ideal for the elixir of the Sun.

the elixir of venus

Lady's mantle or motherwort are good choices for the elixir of Venus. The former (whose Latin name is *Alchemilla*, the "little alchemist") is easily grown in the garden.

the elixir of mercury

Skullcap, caraway, marjoram, or oregano can be used for the elixir of Mercury.

the elixir of the moon

Cheavers is excellent for the elixir of the Moon, but must be used fresh. If cheavers is unavailable, willow bark or chaste-tree berries are good alternatives.

taking the elixirs

When your Jupiter elixir is ready, continue taking the Saturn elixir, but only on Saturdays. Begin taking the Jupiter elixir on the first Thursday of the next New Moon, but only on Thursdays. Do likewise with the other planetary elixirs, taking them in the correct order, as given above.

key points to remember

In all hermetic operations, it is important to bear in mind some key points.

1. Energize yourself through prayer, meditation, or exercise before working. It is important to be calm, but focused, both to avoid making mistakes and to receive profound insights into the nature of the work.

2. Always ensure that your utensils are clean. Glassware should be rinsed with distilled water (or else rainwater) and thoroughly dried.

3. Plants must be positively identified and picked at the right time or purchased from a good source.

4. Always ensure that you work with specific plants on their correct days. This helps to concentrate the planetary energies within the elixir.

GLOSSARY

ALBEDO *The "white" stage of the Great Work. When this stage is reached, the matter is resurrected and it acts as a life-enhancing elixir. It is often symbolized as the White Queen, the White Lion, or the silver Moon.*

ANDROGYNE *As distinct from the hermaphrodite, the androgyne is a human being (or, in alchemical terms, a substance) devoid of either masculine or feminine characteristics.*

APOLLONIUS OF TYANA *Legendary first-century mage, reputed to have discovered the Emerald Tablet in a buried vault.*

BASIL VALENTINE *Thought to be the pseudonymous author of alchemical works. Supposedly an early-fifteenth-century Benedictine monk. His most influential works are* The Twelve Keys *(1599) and* The Triumphal Chariot of Antimony *(1604).*

BYZANTIUM *The old Greek name for Istanbul. Formerly the capital of the Eastern Roman Empire.*

CATHOLIC LEAGUE *An alliance of Catholic realms under the Hapsburg empire, which represented the Counter-Reformation of the Roman Catholic Church. Defeated the Protestant army of Frederick, King of Bohemia in 1620, thus beginning the Thirty Years War between Catholics and Protestants, the bloodiest in Europe prior to World War I.*

CAUDA PAVONIS *The "peacock's tail." A stage in the Great Work characterized by a display of iridescent colors. Always taken as a good sign in the progress toward the Philosopher's Stone.*

CHI *Chinese concept of free energy or life-force contained in the atmosphere, comparable to the alchemical concept of secret or cosmic fire.*

DAO OR TAO *Literally "the Way" or "Path." The central concept of Taoism, an oriental philosophy based on the teachings of Lao Tse. Chinese alchemy is rooted in Taoism.*

FICINO, MARSILIO *Fifteenth-century Italian scholar and philosopher, whose concepts of natural magic, derived mainly from neo-Platonic sources, was highly influential on Renaissance esotericism.*

GNOSTICISM *A religious philosophy based on the concept of gnosis, a belief in the direct spiritual link between man and God, accessible through liberating the divine spark trapped in matter.*

KNIGHTS TEMPLAR *A military religious order founded in the early twelfth century to defend the pilgrimage routes to Jerusalem.*

NEO-PLATONISM *A philosophical system dating from the third century, derived from the work of Plato, Pythagoras, Aristotle, and other esoteric elements. Highly influential in European thought until the thirteenth century and again during the Renaissance.*

NIGREDO *The "black" stage of the Great Work. A destructive, but purifying process associated with philosophical death prior to resurrection.*

NUMEROLOGY *The mystical study of numbers, focusing on the inherent qualities of numbers rather than quantity.*

PRANA *The Indian equivalent of Chi (see above), deriving from Hindu yogic philosophy.*

RUBEDO *The "red" stage of the Great Work, which indicates that the Philosopher's Stone has been successfully perfected. The resulting matter is also called the Red Lion or Red Powder.*

recommended reading

Albertus, Frater, *The Alchemist's Handbook*, Red Wheel/Weiser 1987.

Boehme, Jacob, *Signature of All Things*, Kessinger Publishing Company 1969.

Burckhardt, Titus, *Alchemy: Science of the Cosmos, Science of the Soul*, Fons Vitae 1967.

Eliade, Mircea, *The Forge and the Crucible*, University of Chicago Press 1979.

Evola, Julius, *The Hermetic Tradition: Symbols and Teachings of the Royal Art*, Inner Traditions International Ltd 1994.

Fulcanelli, *The Mystery of the Cathedrals*, Aims International Books 1982.

Fulcanelli, *The Dwellings of the Philosophers*, Archive Press and Communications 2000.

Holmyard, E. J., *Alchemy*, Dover Publications 1957.

Johnson, K.R., *The Fulcanelli Phenomenon*, Spearman (Jersey) 1980.

Jung, C. G., *Psychology and Alchemy*, Princeton University Press 1980.

Junius, Manfred M., *The Practical Handbook of Plant Alchemy*, Robert Heard 1993.

Klossowski de Rola, Stanislas, *Alchemy: The Secret Art*, Thames & Hudson 1973.

Klossowski de Rola, Stanislas, *The Golden Game*, Thames & Hudson 1988.

McLean, Adam, *The Alchemical Engravings of Mylius*, Magnum Opus Hermetic Sourceworks 1984.

McLean, Adam (introduction and commentary) & Godwin, Joscelyn (translation), *The Chemical Wedding of Christian Rosenkreutz*, Magnum Opus Hermetic Sourceworks 1991.

Waite, A. E. (ed), *Hermetical and Alchemical Writings of "Paracelsus" the Great*, Kessinger Publishing Company 1992.

Pernety, Antoine-Joseph, *The Great Art*, 1995.

Read, John, *From Alchemy to Chemistry*, Dover Science Books 1961.

Roberts, Gareth, *The Mirror of Alchemy*, University of Toronto Press 1994.

recommended websites

www.levity.com/alchemy
The Alchemy website contains ninety megabytes of priceless information, articles, scores of original texts, and galleries containing hundreds of alchemical emblems hand-colored by Adam McLean, the world's leading scholar of alchemy.

http://planeta.clix.pt/petrinus
Portuguese alchemist Rubellus Petrinus's website provides some great material on laboratory alchemy for those who want to become more serious.

www.paxprofundis.com/parush/index.html
The Alchemist's Garret offers articles, original texts, and useful lab notes.

www.triad-publishing.com/index.html
The Philosophers of Nature website offers excellent study courses on spagyrics and the cabala.

www.spagyria.com
Spagyria is the website of John Reid III, spagyrist and philosopher.

INDEX